The 10 Commandments Of Friendship

Jerome & Marla McCarthy

The 10 Commandments of Friendship
Copyright © 2011 by Jerome J. McCarthy & Marla A. McCarthy

Published by The Real Life Series Publishing Co., LLC.
All Rights Reserved.

ISBN-10: 0-9800083-6-0
ISBN-13: 978-0-9800083-6-4

No part of this book may be reproduced or transmitted in any form or by any means electronic or mechanical – including photocopying, recording, or by any information storage and retrieval system – without permission in writing from the publisher. Please direct your inquiries to permissions@thereallifeseries.com

First Printing August 2013

Concept by Marla A. McCarthy
Graphic Design and typesetting by Jerome J. McCarthy

Inquires should be addressed to:
The Real Life Series Publishing Co., LLC
PO BOX 1563
Keller, TX 76244-1896

www.TheRealLifeSeries.com
info@thereallifeseries.com

*This book is dedicated
to the loving memories of our mothers,
Deborah Hollins & Linda McCarthy,
whose giving spirits and selfless acts taught us about
true love and relationships.*

TABLE OF CONTENTS

INTRODUCTION / 3
ACQUAINTANCES VS. FRIENDS / 7
40 GOOD FRIEND CHARACTERISTICS / 11
40 BAD FRIEND CHARACTERISTICS / 17
COMMANDMENT I / 25
COMMANDMENT II / 43
COMMANDMENT III / 57
COMMANDMENT IV / 67
COMMANDMENT V / 79
COMMANDMENT VI / 89
COMMANDMENT VII / 107
COMMANDMENT VIII / 117
COMMANDMENT IX / 129
COMMANDMENT X / 137
CONCLUSION / 151

10 COMMANDMENTS OF FRIENDSHIP
Introduction

Introduction

Friendship...is not something you learn in school. But if you haven't learned the meaning of friendship, you really haven't learned anything.
~Muhammad Ali

To navigate successfully through life it is essential to learn how to manage relationships. Discovering how to conduct ourselves in relationships is vitally important to keeping quality individuals a part of our lives. For friendships to be successful we must be taught how to interact with others. But first, we must define what friendship means. Oftentimes we use the term loosely with those we socialize with regularly, but what is a friend?

A friend is a valued or favored companion. They are someone you desire to interact and spend your time with above all the other people you meet and know. These are the people who you develop a more intimate relationship with than other individuals with who you are simply acquainted. A friend may be someone you connect with and see on a regular basis. Or it could be someone you don't speak to or see everyday, but you both are there for one another when it counts.

The purpose of friendships in our lives is to provide us with companionship and support on our life journey. The people we choose to be friends with are usually those with who we are united through some of the same interests, a common purpose, or cause. Friends are those who we desire to bond with, support, give to, and help along their life journey. We also appreciate their presence and cherish their support throughout our life.

Friendships contribute greatly to our life experience and can be an extremely valuable part of our existence. Some of us have experienced amazing highs in life as result of our friendships and many of us have also suffered major disappointments. Therefore once we develop a great friendship, we should appreciate it and view it as a great treasure. Through times of disappointment, we foster an understanding that a true friendship is rare and worth maintaining.

The 10 Commandments of Friendship is an insightful resource that informs us of what to do and what not to do in order to begin, develop, maintain and repair a friendship. These guidelines within will assist you in learning how to step outside of your circumstances in order to be a better friend to others. You will learn the importance in your willingness to give versus being anxious to take, and how to demonstrate love instead of manifesting envy. Until you understand your role in friendship and how to conduct yourself, you will never fully experience the entire blessing of having, or more importantly being a friend.

There are different dynamics to people's friendships and their needs during the various stages and seasons of life. At times you may need a listening ear, or shoulder to lean or cry on. Other times you may need someone to make you laugh. There are seasons in life when you may need someone to pray with and for you, or when you may just need a hug, affection, or simple touch to remind you that everything is going to be alright. There are some circumstances that call for someone to love you enough to be completely honest and truthful about what is occurring in your life to protect you from your own disastrous choices. These are periods of time when you need someone to counsel you or give you wisdom and advice on how to improve, enhance or repair your current situation. Then there are days or moments that come when you need someone to simply, *silently* sit beside you.

It is very important to understand that in order for

INTRODUCTION

friendships to be lasting and successful, they require a high level of faith and expectancy for your own life. If you do not possess a high level of faith and expectancy for your own life, you will more than likely do something destructive in your friendship as a result of your own unhappiness, discontentment or lack of faith for what is possible for your future. Wavering faith makes it challenging for you to be supportive during the times of achievement and victory in your friends' lives.

In order to refrain from initiating destructive actions in your friendships, you must absolutely trust that great things are possible for you. You must develop wisdom and the peace of knowing that positive experiences will be a part of your future. Changing your perception and increasing your faith will prevent you from doing something hurtful to your friends during their moments of triumph, or seasons of harvest and celebration.

Once you appreciate that God's plan and purpose for your life is unique, good, and custom-ordered specifically for you, then you will be less likely to become jealous or envious of others, attempt to control others, and destroy the friendships you currently have. Confidence for your own amazing life will enable you to be the best person that you can be. A strong level of faith will give you the ability to strengthen the relationships you have been blessed with, and maintain the ones you develop in the future.

If you want friends, you have to learn how to be a friend first. People are more likely to make time for the positive, uplifting people in their life. In order to build and maintain friendships, you need to be the type of person that people want to be around. To accomplish that you must be what you want others to be in your life, and also learn to treat others how *they* want to be treated.

THE 10 COMMANDMENTS OF FRIENDSHIP

Look outside of yourself and see what *their* situation is and what *their* needs are at the moment. It is great to treat others how you want to be treated, but it is even better to acknowledge what someone is going through and be what they need during that season of their life.

Friendships definitely have ups and downs, good days and not so good days. Your friends are not going to be perfect, and neither are you. But if you can learn how to forgive, apologize, and develop the other skills necessary to be a better friend to others, your relationships can last through the more challenging moments and seasons of life.

Oftentimes life becomes so challenging and overwhelming that we tend to dismiss how precious and important relationships are. *The 10 Commandments of Friendship* is a guide which serves as a reminder that friendships are valuable, crucial to growth, and must be nurtured to last. It will provide highly useful insights on how to establish and maintain friendships that will enrich your life.

Use these commandments as a self-reflective tool to honestly assess your past relationships, examine your current friendships, or possibly consider the reasons your friendships are lacking. As you navigate through the pages of this book, you will inevitably see characteristics of yourself and others you know or interact with daily. Focus on what you can do to become a better friend and enhance the relationships in your life. Answer the questions at the end of each chapter, and take action. As a result, you will be more capable of building, strengthening, or repairing your relationships, and will have the knowledge necessary to have lasting friendships far exceeding any experience you have ever known!

10 Commandments of Friendship
Acquaintances vs. Friends

ACQUAINTANCES VS. FRIENDS

A real friend is someone who would feel loss if you jumped on a train, or in front of one.
~Author Unknown

When you meet someone, it doesn't necessarily mean they will become your friend. There are some people that may fall into the acquaintance category. This is a gray undefined area for some. There are times when you may consider someone a friend and they do not share the same view. Similarly, someone can see you as a friend while you may view them as someone you just pass by on a regular basis. For the purpose of future discussions, let's specifically define an acquaintance verses a friend.

Friendship is driven by perception. It is based on the manner in which *both* individuals perceive the relationship. A friend is someone you have a deep knowledge of, fondness for, a strong bond, and life experiences with. Conversely, an acquaintance is someone who you simply have knowledge of. You can mutually choose to build friendships after being acquaintances. However, having mere knowledge of a person though or a few minor details of their life does not automatically make you two friends. If an individual is not a person you share the more intimate details of your life with, or the person you would call when you experience an extreme loss or disappointment in your life, then it is likely they are not your friend.

Sometimes this may be hard to discern as you may know of numerous people or view someone as a more important person in your life than they view you. The problematic issue of two individuals having different perceptions is that you may be demanding friendship qualities from others when they only consider you an acquaintance. When assessing your relationship, you cannot assume the person in question feels the same way about you that you feel about them. Time, trials, and life experiences together will show you who your friends are and who they are not.

A friend will be there during your most challenging, painful times in life. A friend is someone you have an intimate, cherished relationship with. Friends support you in the important moments; whether they are the highs or lows. They are likely someone with whom you are united in a cause, who assists you in your life purpose, and you are committed to encouraging and assisting them in theirs. Before you begin to work on your friendships, make sure that you are not in the friendship alone.

If you desire to be someone's friend, be patient and give them time to get to know you, appreciate your presence, and warm up to building a friendship with you. Be kind, empathetic, considerate and demonstrate love to others realizing that building friendships and trust takes time. You should always show yourself friendly in order to gain friends. Just understand that your friendliness may not always be appreciated or reciprocated.

It is also important to acknowledge when someone desires to maintain their position as an acquaintance. By discerning your role, it will enable you to spend your time more wisely on relationships that are enhancing your life and building you up, rather than those that may be harmful and destructive. There are certain characteristics that should give you an indication on whether to continue in the relationship, or open yourself up to building new ones with others. The following pages will assist you in assessing good and bad friend character traits.

10 COMMANDMENTS OF FRIENDSHIP
40 Good Friend Characteristics

40 Good Friend Characteristics

From time to time it is necessary to evaluate your friendships. Are the individuals you are spending time with good friends to you? Use this list below to assess not only your friends, but also to examine how good of a friend you are to others. If someone in your life possesses most of these qualities, then you have found someone rare that you need to cherish, appreciate, care for, and hold dear to your heart.

40 Good Friend Characteristics…

1. You can trust that they will follow through on what they say.

2. You trust that they will keep their mouth shut about your personal life and business.

3. They do not misuse or abuse intimate details you share with them.

4. They respect and are considerate of your time.

5. They check on you every now and then.

6. They respect your emotional boundaries and physical space.

7. They genuinely have your best interest at heart.

8. They are always trying to sow positive words and experiences into your life.

9. They are more concerned about what they can give to you than what they can get or snatch from you.

The 10 Commandments Of Friendship

10. They respect and value your thoughts, words, and opinions.

11. They are encouraging and uplifting.

12. They help you to believe in yourself, your goals and your dreams.

13. You can learn positive information and glean wisdom from them.

14. They are giving, loving, compassionate and caring in all relationships of their life.

15. Your interaction with them is causing you to grow in a positive way.

16. Your life is improved as a result of their presence.

17. They are empathetic and supportive in the changes and seasons of your life, and are accepting of your growth.

18. They are open to learning and growing in life.

19. They enrich your life. You feel stronger and more courageous as a result of their presence.

20. They are there for you during the good times *and* bad times.

21. They enjoy connecting with, talking to, and spending time with you. And you feel the same about them.

22. The person is kind-hearted and loyal.

23. Your interaction with them increases your self-

esteem.

24. The relationship (or your interaction) energizes you and brings you joy.

25. They accept and love who you are, but are also willing to tell you the truth in love to help you grow.

26. They give you room, time and space to live and grow.

27. They are trustworthy, honest and genuine.

28. You share a common bond, purpose or common interests.

29. They are willing to accept responsibility when they mess up or make mistakes in life.

30. They speak loving, kind, uplifting words into your life and spirit about your goals and dreams.

31. They inspire you to become a better person through how they live their own life.

32. Their presence is refreshing. You feel better when you leave them than when you arrived.

33. You receive wise counsel and advice from them.

34. They look out, protect, or keep an eye out for danger for you.

35. They lovingly attempt to keep you from making wrong turns, traveling down paths that go nowhere, or heeding bad advice from those who are

The 10 Commandments Of Friendship

obviously lost themselves.

36. You two can laugh together or they can make you laugh.

37. They celebrate your triumphs and achievements with you.

38. They are present in your life whether you are wealthy, popular and famous, or unknown without two nickels to rub together.

39. Your life is more peaceful and enjoyable as a result of their presence.

40. You feel blessed for knowing them.

10 COMMANDMENTS OF FRIENDSHIP
―――――――――――――――――
40 Bad Friend Characteristics

40 Bad Friend Characteristics

Some friends have a negative impact on our lives. As we grow and mature, it is necessary to analyze the state of our relationships and the company we keep. We must at times evaluate whether the people in our lives are helpful or hurtful to our well-being and goals for our future.

If a person in your life possesses many of the negative characteristics listed below, it may be time to move on and end the relationship until that ratio of bad to good characteristics changes. Use these lists as a starting point to assess your relationship and insure your friendship is not toxic or damaging to the quality of your life.

As you regularly assess the state of your friendships, you should also critically analyze your own behavior to see why you may be attracting people with these issues listed below. If you read the list below and find one or more of these negative characteristics apply to you, fix it. There is no need to overanalyze it or make excuses. Simply stop doing it. These types of behaviors repel good people and good life experiences from you. Change to improve your own quality of life.

40 Bad Friend Characteristics…

1. They habitually lie.

2. Your relationship or interaction drains and sucks the life out of you.

3. They can't hold water. In other words, they are always telling your business to everyone.

4. They are unsupportive.

5. They are jealous or possessive.

The 10 Commandments Of Friendship

6. They throw temper tantrums or attempt to put others on punishment when they do not get their way.

7. They talk you into doing something unwise, stupid or foolish. Usually to make themselves feel better about the unwise, stupid or foolish things they've done.

8. They try to convince you to do something your conscience makes you feel really uncomfortable about or something to taint your integrity.

9. They pursue or accept the advances of your significant other or spouse (or your ex- significant other or spouse) even if you say it is okay. This is a sign of selfishness as there are millions of other people in the world they could develop a relationship with.

10. They seem to be upset with you when you advance in your life, when you experience a good harvest, or for putting in necessary work to get what you have and where you are.

11. They always take, take, take, take, and take some more.

12. They won't ever shut up, they never listen and they rarely or never ask how you are doing.

13. They only call you to dump all their issues/burdens on you, and then get off the phone.

14. They only call you to see what your status is to gauge themselves, try to one-up you, or attempt

to destroy you.

15. If their words, actions, or advice are causing your life to move in a negative direction, placing you in danger, or encouraging you to engage in any harmful behavior or illegal activity.

16. They don't want anything about you or your life to ever grow or change.

17. The friendship is very one-sided. You are the only one ever giving.

18. They are there for you only during times that are convenient for them.

19. The person is avoiding you.

20. The individual is outright mean, a bully, negative, or passive-aggressive.

21. They only care about what is going on in their life.

22. They believe rumors and gossip about you without talking to you about it.

23. They are conniving and start rumors against you behind your back.

24. Your interaction and conversations with this person leave you feeling down on yourself, or decrease your self-esteem.

25. They must control or be in charge of everything.

26. They desire or attempt to consume all of your

The 10 Commandments Of Friendship

time (and energy).

27. They are competitive to the point of damaging your relationship.

28. They are angry and bitter in their everyday life and interactions with you and others.

29. They can never accept responsibility for anything that happens in their life or that they do to others.

30. They are toxic to not only your life, but possibly themselves and almost everything they touch.

31. They don't ever get back to you when you contact or reach out to them.

32. They are physically, verbally, or emotionally abusive.

33. They could care less about you, and how you feel.

34. You feel worse when you leave their presence than when you arrived.

35. They take you down life paths with them that lead nowhere or to a dead-end.

36. They assume they already know everything about life.

37. They only come around if you can do something for them, then they abandon you when things get tough.

38. They expect you to be generous when they are

stingy.

39. They are fickle. You have to walk on egg shells because you never know what personality or emotional state you are going to get.

40. You feel worse off for having ever met them.

Commandment I
Thou shalt respect boundaries

Commandment I:
Thou shalt respect boundaries

I don't need a friend who changes when I change and who nods when I nod; my shadow does that much better.
~Plutarch

The purpose of a boundary is to limit or protect a person or thing. Friendship boundaries are essentially safety precautions for your emotional and physical well-being. When these boundaries are crossed or not adhered to, the results can be disastrous.

In order to operate an automobile, one must prove they can adhere to traffic laws and maneuver within boundaries such as yellow and white road markings, guardrails, and signs. These laws and boundaries were put in place to allow us to safely drive within our own lane and to navigate successfully. When these laws and boundaries are ignored, it could lead to permanent damage, physical injury, or possibly the loss of life.

In the same way physical boundaries protect us from harm, we must also implement relationship boundaries so we can navigate through life effectively. These boundaries serve a major purpose and are needed in order for friendships to be healthy and long-lasting.

Personal, emotional and physical boundaries need to be established in order to protect time and energy for yourself, your loved ones, and your goals. Unfortunately no one cares about your time more than you. The reality is there are people in the world who will consume all of your time, energy and resources if you allow them. They will completely drain all the life and creativity out of you if you do not put boundaries in place to ensure that it does not happen.

The 10 Commandments Of Friendship

When boundaries aren't in place or when they are crossed, people find themselves growing resentful towards their friends. This resentment emanates from being passive and not speaking up regarding the situation that is bothering you. By simply standing your ground about boundaries you have in place for your own life, even if it makes someone uncomfortable, you will prevent the slow erosion of your friendship.

When you are a true friend you allow (not demand) others to give you their time, attention, resources and use of their gifts at their leisure and willingness. You don't try to force it, and you do not throw temper tantrums when you don't get what you want. You also should make every effort possible to display your appreciation for whatever someone gives or contributes to your life, positive emotional state, life purpose, or cause.

The term *boundary* is a broad term as its definition could vary by person. The following are just a few common basic building blocks for friendship boundaries:

- Respect your friend's time
- Respect your friend's bubble (or physical space)
- Respect your friend's friendships with others
- Respect your friend's relationship with their spouse or significant other
- Respect your friend's right to manage their resources how they see fit

Respect their time...

Time is precious commodity and probably the most important boundary. It is one of the few things in life you cannot retrieve once it has been lost. Money, jobs, opportunities or anything material can literally be here today, gone tomorrow. But once time is lost, it is gone forever.

Our time on this earth is consumed by the pursuit of various personal goals. We at times measure our happiness by these goals we set and the success we have at achieving benchmarks in life. Since we are not immortal and our time will eventually run out, the manner in which we spend or waste our time becomes very important.

One of the greatest ways that you can show someone that you love and care about them is to be respectful of their time. It is one thing if you two are mutually making plans, enjoying your time together, and have nothing pressing to do. However, one of the most annoying things a friend can do is absorb and waste your time by making plans for you, without any consideration for what you already had going on, only taking into consideration what they desire to do.

To build strong, lasting, enjoyable relationships and friendships you must have a high regard for and esteem the time, physical, and emotional boundaries of your friends. Consider their boundaries before you act, make requests or speak to them. Ask them if they are busy before you dive into what you want. When you respect the time and boundaries of others, you will receive a more favorable response than if you do not.

Make it possible for them to enjoy when they give or sow time and resources into your life, instead of causing it feel like a chore or obligation. You can make requests from your friends, but consider what is going on in their life as well before you make your request. More importantly, give them time, space, room and opportunity to decide for their selves what they want to do, give or participate in. Try not to make requesting something from your friends a constant part of your interaction with one another or they may start avoiding you. Think about what you are really asking from them and be grateful when they decide to give of themselves or their resources. Always remember, no one in life owes you anything. Then you will be appreciative and able to conduct yourself in a manner becoming of a great friend.

To be respectful of your friend's time requires you to be unselfish and think outside of yourself. It is possible to check on others without invading too much of their time. Give them a brief call to see how they are doing, versus calling to dump all your problems on them. Drop by for a short visit, but only after you have called first to make sure that it is okay and a good time. Do not just show up and expect people to be accepting and welcoming of your presence. If you do that one too many times you are likely to never hear from that person again. There may be a situation where a call or brief visit is not possible at the time, so shoot an e-mail message or text to say "hello" or "how are you?" At this point, most people will let you know what is going on with them and what they do or do not have time for. You can then plan your life, events, outings and time with your friends accordingly.

If you find yourself wanting to charge into someone else's life, space, and time - don't. Learn to be patient and wait for them to invite you into those areas of their life. Understand that if they don't have a lot of time or resources available right now to give to you or to your cause, that another season of their life in the future may open up opportunities for you to spend more time together. Let them do what is necessary to get through this period of their life and build to a point where they may be able to be more involved in what you desire. You possibly may go through a similar season that they are experiencing one day, so don't criticize and be considerate. If you choose otherwise, understand that life has a way of causing you to be quiet and less judgemental of others.

Give your friends space as they need it, and don't get offended by everything they will not or cannot do. One of the most important lessons you can learn in being a friend to others is that *everything is not always about you*. Other people have challenges, wants, desires, goals, problems and life experiences they are coping and dealing with as well. Open your eyes and heart up to what may be happening to the people you call your friends.

Respect their bubble...

Your friend's bubble is the personal physical space around their physical body. It may come as a surprise, but some people do not like to touch noses or physically breathe the carbon dioxide released from the person who they are having a conversation with. If you are a touchy feely person, do not assume the person you are conversing with is. A general rule is to not get within arm's reach of someone unless or until their body language or verbal response invites you in further.

Being considerate of someone's personal space keeps people from having the urge to literally run from you when you come around to avoid being in an uncomfortable position. It does not mean you can't physically demonstrate your love, care and affection for your friends. If you are a touchy feely person, simply give your new friends an opportunity to warm up to and get to know you better before diving in and wrapping your arms around them. Also, realize that they still may not desire to have you in their bubble then, so don't be offended. Try to pay attention to the culture, body language and response of people concerning what you do and say around them. Your friendships will be the better for it.

Respect their friendships with others...

THE 10 COMMANDMENTS OF FRIENDSHIP

People have the ability to be friends with more than one person. Getting offended at your friend having other friends is a sure fire way to begin to erode or destroy your friendship. It is an emotion rooted in fear which oftentimes has no bearing on your relationship until you harbor it and allow your insecurities to manifest into destructive actions.

There are many reasons people can give as to why a particular person is their friend. Some people like how supportive their friend is. Others are fond of the way their friend makes them laugh and the fun they have together. Your friend may at some point develop a friendship with someone who has traits you may not exhibit. This is not a shot towards you, nor does it diminish your relationship. It may just have something to do with their current season, a life experience they have in common, or it may be the type of relationship or person they need in their life at the time.

People tend to gravitate to those who can understand their plight. It is normal healthy human behavior that we connect to those who have familiar circumstances such as relationship status (married or single), parenting, not having children, health concerns, education or profession to name a few. Therefore when a new friend is introduced, try not to think of it like you are being replaced. You still have a very important role in their life and place in their heart, and more than likely they still want and desire you in their life as well. Faced with this situation, it is best to just be who you are, fulfill your role, and be there for your friend when they need you.

If the situation appears to be toxic and you see that your friend is in harm's way, first take a step back and assess if there may be a tinge of jealousy driving your emotions. Learn to be silent and carefully observe before you speak. Ultimately the best way to deal with these situations is to give your friend their space and privacy, allow them to make their own decisions and still remain supportive. Whatever is harmful to the life of your friend from that relationship will be revealed without your help as the truth always reveals itself. It's not that you can't bring up your concerns, but be careful that what you are saying is honest, truthful, and for the right or unselfish reasons.

Do not interrupt or become envious of your friends when they network, intermingle or communicate with others. If you find yourself having these emotions, ask yourself why? What do you feel you are losing or lacking? What are you fearful of in that very moment that is causing you to have a negative reaction about your friend interacting with and befriending other people?

You don't have to verbally discuss it, but you do need to pause, ask yourself these questions, and address the issues in your own life. By taking a few moments to be honest with yourself, you may keep yourself from doing or saying something to hurt, harm or destroy your current friendship. Figure out what is bothering you, avoid being invasive in the life of your friend, and choose to spend your energy on taking positive actions toward getting or achieving what you want for your own life. Doing so will save many relationships as you move forward into your future.

Respect their relationship with their significant other…

The Past - Relationships with spouses or significant others can be huge obstacles for many friendships. Jealousy and envy can quickly interrupt a friendship if the individuals in the friendship are not experiencing love and happiness in this area of life at the same time.

The 10 Commandments Of Friendship

The first boundary in your friendships concerning this topic is a long-standing, unwritten rule that the "ex" is off limits. This rule exists to prevent complicated, uncomfortable, possibly hurtful situations. Yet people still allow loneliness, self-centered desires, desperation, and possibly the lure and excitement of a new relationship to entice them into ignoring this much needed boundary and leaping into these many times likely disastrous circumstances.

If your friend pursues or accepts the advances of your significant other or spouse, or your ex-significant other or ex-spouse, it is a sign of selfishness and that your friendship has dropped on their list of priorities. It sadly sends the message that their immediate desires are more important than your friendship and your feelings are irrelevant.

If you are in a situation where you are allured by your friend's ex and your friend verbally gives you permission to date them, it is still not a wise decision. Regardless of how their relationship ended, how ridiculously attracted to this person you are or you how you vibe in every way, understand that it is never okay. It is a very difficult emotion to cope with and too touchy of a situation for a true friend to exploit. If the relationship progresses, that choice makes the friendship uncomfortable going forward as the element of distrust is introduced.

Can a friendship survive this? Yes, it is possible but unlikely. A situation like this will be more destructive than productive for your friendship. It is most times more destructive than the individuals in the friendship could ever predict or forecast. Whether the friend states it or not, they will more than likely feel betrayed and your selfish decision will always be at the forefront of their mind. If you love and care for your friend and want to keep or maintain a good friendship, you won't go there!

The Present/Future – It is difficult when you have a friend who is dating someone, and you're the third wheel. So simply put, don't be the third wheel. Give your friend space to explore whether this relationship is worth advancing in. It is a challenging time, but your friend will have more respect for you if you are supportive and allow them space to explore a relationship, versus being the one that tries to interfere or break them up.

You must also understand that this person may potentially be their spouse one day, so be cautious of the words you say and try to remain positive. It does not mean you can't share your honest opinion, it just means be wise about the words you speak. If you are single and your friend's relationship progresses to marriage, it adds a different dynamic to your friendship. You can still remain friends, but you should not expect your friend to act as if they are single just because you are.

If you are the married friend and your friends are encouraging you to still act or carry yourself as if you are single, this is a problem. If you desire to have a healthy, long-lasting, love-filled marriage, you may need to seriously reassess or possibly back away from or end those friendships. That is if you cherish your spouse and care about their feelings, and your desire is not to end up in divorce court.

If you do not have a friend or friends who fully support your marital relationship, it becomes problematic for you all to hang out frequently as you now have different interests and are temporarily on different paths. In other words, if you are single, this is not the season in the life of your married friend for you to encourage them to act like they are single, or put them in compromising situations in various locations like a club or bar.

The 10 Commandments Of Friendship

The truth is that many of these establishments have many patrons whose intentions are to meet someone, hook-up or have their daily attention quotas filled by others. One challenging day or argument in the marital relationship of your friend could possibly lead to a bad choice, major trouble, irreparable damage, or the destruction of their marriage. There is no good that can come to your friend by encouraging them to act like they are single. You must understand there is a difference between what's fun or you want your friend to do, and what is best for your friend's life, marital relationship, and future.

Choose not to be destructive in their life just because they have entered a new season that you may not have entered into with them. Think about what it really means to be a true friend in this situation and be that. It doesn't mean you two can't hang out by any means. It just means you need to truly assess your intentions, and the possible consequences or repercussions of your possible actions within the locations you choose to hang out in, prior to something disastrous occurring.

Your married friends may have an urge to participate in activities that are hurtful to their spouse or marriage, just because it is momentarily fun or providing attention for them. Or they may have a desire in their heart and mind to say no, but you utilize playground peer pressure to convince them into walking away from their conscious. If you are considering what is in the best interest of your friend's life and other people their decisions affect (e.g. spouse, children, extended family), then you will not encourage them to behave in an unfaithful manner.

Many marriages have been destroyed as a result of married individuals attempting to hold onto their past single lives. Is it totally their friends' faults? Absolutely not. However you can choose as a friend to not be an encouraging factor in their harmful behavior and infidelity. Anytime you put someone in a situation where they want to say no but don't feel as if they can in an attempt to be nice or salvage your friendship, you are not being the best friend you can be.

When you encourage your married friend to act single, you exhibit selfishness and discontentment with your own life choices. It becomes all about what you want, and you could care less about the consequences of the actions you set in motion. If you put your friends in situations when you know the potential outcome could be disastrous to their relationship, you reveal you don't care what happens to their spouse, children or their future. The only thing that truly matters is what you want when you want it. Your friend will be left to put the broken pieces of their life together after a divorce; meanwhile you are still partying and enjoying your life.

A good friend is not destructive, nor do they plant seeds of dissension within another's marriage. A good friend will take a step back and be respectful of the relationship their friend has consciously chosen to be in, and of the time it takes to cultivate it. They will encourage their friend to spend time with their family, accept their new supportive role in the friendship and understand that their friendship now has to take a backseat to their friend's marriage. This is a new season of their life and adjustments must be made for them to be successful at this season and endeavor.

Is this easy? Probably not, but it is absolutely necessary in order to be a good friend. In doing so, your friendship can remain intact even though the dynamics and roles have changed. Friendships are like old building renovations. If there is a good foundation and structure, oftentimes you can leave the building intact and just redesign it. By simply respecting their relationship, being an encouraging factor in their faithfulness to their mate, and redefining/restructuring your role, you can place yourself to be among the few people who can state they have successful friendships that last through multiple decades and life experiences.

Respect their resources…

Life at times can be difficult. Along this journey, we all take different paths to what we perceive will lead to our ultimate happiness. Whether it is personal business, a specific career, or a job in the workforce, we socialize and attempt to network in order to make connections, gain an advantage and financial benefits. In doing this, we may find that our life or career path may take a different turn from a friend. When this happens we should recognize it and continue to be supportive and encouraging as your season for success and opportunities can arrive one day as well as you work toward your goals.

Your friend's choice of path is just as important as yours. Their goals are just as important as yours. This is not the time to become bitter, or try to leach and siphon all of your friend's resources, acquaintances or connections. Your friend should be able to share resources with you because they care about you, not because they feel obligated or pressured. This is another situation which places them in an awkward position to say no. Be respectful of their resources and connections with others as they strive to reach their goals. Use your own time, energy and resources to create the life you desire for yourself. Can you and your friends help one another out? Yes! Do they have to give you their time, resources, and connections? No. So be grateful and appreciative of when they do. Tell them thank you, send a card, a gift, or provide them with a nice meal to show your appreciation for what they have done for you. Remember, no one in life owes you anything. They can give into your life as they choose to do so, but they are not obligated.

Resources don't necessarily have to be physical or tangible items, but they could be your talents. There are many cases where friends exploit the talents of another friend for their own benefit. This infringes upon the time boundary as well. It can be really challenging to find the balance between giving to others, sowing into the lives of others around you, and finding the time, resources and energy to reach your own life goals and dreams.

Since most individuals do not have infinite resources and time, we all can struggle at times with balancing being a good friend and supporter with taking care of our own goals, wants and needs. It can become overwhelming, but take a breath and learn to take life one moment and day at a time. In an attempt to foster relationships, try to be as loving, caring and giving as possible. Relationships truly are the most important aspect of life. Learn and know your limits, and set boundaries so that you don't stretch yourself thin. Your true friends will understand your life circumstances, your aspirations, as well as your desire to be there for them.

When boundaries are not respected…

Everyone was not raised with loving boundaries in place on their behavior. One look at the workplace, youth sporting event, church or any place where adults congregate and you will see immature behavior similar to that of a grade school child. Just because someone is adult in age doesn't mean they are an adult in behavior or mind-set, nor does it mean they can discern your boundaries. There are individuals around you who struggle with human relationships as a result of their behavior and way of thinking. They are usually overbearing, obnoxious and clueless as to why people have no desire to be around them.

If you have someone who is not respecting your life boundaries, sit down and discuss the issue you are having with them and what is going on that is causing you to need some space or breathing room. If they get angry, won't listen, and still will not respect your boundaries, you may have to distance yourself from them for this moment, time or season until something changes in your life where you can cope with them.

You very well may have to outright back away for a brief period until they decide to make a change and become a more considerate person. They are likely becoming angry with you because what they want at the moment is more important to them than what you are going through. But you must ask yourself, is that the definition or role of a friend? You can be a giving person and be as supportive and celebrant of your friends as possible, but you should not make your life all about pleasing people and trying to prevent temper tantrums of emotionally and spiritually immature friends.

At times when someone is not being the best friend or being a friend at all during a trial you are going through, you may need to back up, take a break, and protect your life, health, mental stability, resources, emotional state, and spiritual strength to make it through this season. If the friends in your life do not understand when you clearly attempt to explain what your trials and current needs are, then let that be their problem. They probably weren't that great or true of a friend to begin with, and it probably will not be a major loss to your life. True, loving, enduring friends will understand when you need a little time and space to regroup, cope with life, or time to work on your goals and dreams.

So how do you more easily respect the boundaries of others? When you develop and work toward goals and a life of your own, you will be more likely to respect the time, resources, skills, gifts, abilities, and boundaries of others. Having life experiences and goals of your own to spend your time on will cause you to have a greater appreciation for and understanding of the various seasons, changes, and challenges that may be occurring in your friend's lives.

You alone know what your boundaries and limits are. Protect those boundaries and don't allow other inconsiderate people to cross them. Acknowledge and respect the boundaries and limits of your friends as well. You should know, understand, and discuss with your friends the extent, range, or degree beyond which you both may not proceed without causing damage to or the destruction of your relationship.

Non-communicated issues are the most destructive to relationships. You may do something to cause a relationship to end without even understanding what you've done if you two do not openly and honestly communicate about what your physical and emotional boundaries are. Don't bicker or complain about what the boundaries of your friends are. Express your feelings and opinions, and then calmly make choices and decisions for your own life. Bickering and complaining disrupts, destroys, and hinders friendships. A positive tone and frame of mind will open up and pave a way for your friendships to grow and thrive. If you appreciate the value and worth of your friendship, you will respect the boundaries your friend has for their life.

If you want to rebuild a relationship with someone who you have overstepped your boundaries with and caused them to end the relationship or avoid you, consider simply checking on them, dropping them a note, quick call or a message to see how they are doing. When you do so, be prepared to give them time, room, space, space, and more space to respond.

It is refreshing and heart-warming when others check on you, so it may open the door back up to restore the friendship. If not, consider it a lesson learned and don't overstep your boundaries with the next individual that allows you to be a part of their life. Learning how to set boundaries of your own and accept the boundaries that others set, is the framework, foundation, and a necessary step in developing strong, lasting, enjoyable friendships.

Questions:
- What are your boundaries?
- What are the boundaries of your friends? If they have not communicated them to you, what can you observe about their life that you may need to be more considerate of?
- How can you do better at respecting the time, emotional, and physical boundaries of your friends?
- Who do you need to do better with in this area?
- Who in your life do you wish was more respectful of your time and boundaries? When and how can you lovingly communicate and discuss this issue with them?

Commandment II
Thou shalt celebrate achievements

Commandment II:
Thou shalt celebrate achievements

A friendship can weather most things and thrive in thin soil; but it needs a little mulch of letters and phone calls and small, silly presents every so often - just to save it from drying out completely.
~Pam Brown

A true friend will be genuinely happy and joyous for the good experiences, events, and accomplishments in your life. A successful friendship requires give and take in this area. If you want someone to celebrate you, then you have to be supportive and celebrate them in return. Simply put, you cannot expect for others to show up for your events, achievements and milestones and then never show up for theirs. You cannot neglect, ignore, be jealous or outright act ugly about the positive activities, accomplishments and events in friends' lives, then expect to maintain healthy, strong, long-lasting friendships.

The following list reflects a few good experiences, days, events, and accomplishments that you should acknowledge or celebrate with your friends…

Good Life Experiences:
- Birthdays
- Anniversaries
- Graduations
- Weddings
- Holidays
- Mother's day
- Father's day
- The birth of children or an adoption
- When they achieve something honorable, note-

worthy, or receive an award
- When they feel loved or find someone to love
- When the good they put out into the world comes back to them in some manner
- When they experience favor
- When they develop further skills or obtain additional education
- When they are promoted or start a new business venture
- When they build new relationships
- When they grow spiritually
- When they have their wants, needs or desires met
- When they are healthy or recover from an illness
- When they overcome an obstacle
- When they accomplish a major personal goal
- When they demonstrate emotional, spiritual, or physical strength in their life and when they grow in each of these areas

It is easy for you to be in high spirits during these moments of your friends' life when you understand that the same (or something different/bigger) is attainable for your own life. In other words, the level of faith you exhibit for what is possible for your own life regulates your behavior towards your friends' accomplishments.

Take time to observe the important dates, events, achievements and positive experiences of your friends' lives. Rejoice with your friends as often as you can. These are the most precious moments in life to your friend, but they also enrich your life as well. These experiences create positive memories that you will reflect on years later; and possibly will regret if you miss them.

Be glad for the good in the lives of those who are important to you and those whose path you cross along your life journey. Pause and allow yourself to feel a sense of joy for what is happening in their lives. Take pleasure in their prosperity, rather than fearing that you won't be able to prosper and have good life experiences of your own.

Fear makes strangers of people who would be friends.
~Shirley MacLaine

Fear eliminates the opportunity to gain new friends and limits your ability to strengthen relationships with people in your life. Most people attempt to mask their fears, but do not realize fear is the silent catalyst to the destruction of many friendships. If you have anxiety about what you don't have or what you think you may lose as a result of your friend's success and good fortune, then you need to learn how to address your fears.

To manage fear, action is required with a spirit of power, love, and sound mind. Whenever you have the inability to be happy for and celebrate others, set aside a moment for introspection. During this meditative time, think through what it is you may fear, be overwhelmed about, or feel you are lacking in your own life. After you discern the culprit of your fear, use the love in your heart and sound mind that God has blessed you with to *do* something about it.

Get occupied with fulfilling your own life purpose so that you can be happy for others when they are accomplishing theirs. Don't use any of your energy or brain power to hate, sabotage, or wish harm on anyone. Imagine what you could accomplish with your life if you poured all of the energy you may have wasted on being envious and hateful into doing something much more positive with your time.

The 10 Commandments Of Friendship

If you have a friend that exercises frequently, eats healthy, and does all the other things it takes to be physically fit, you cannot be mad that their physique is better than yours; especially when you were not willing to put in the effort. You can be mad, but it will not change your physique. You are responsible for your own body, goals, and dreams. Your level of faith and what you believe you can have for your life is nobody else's responsibility. You have to take ownership in raising your level of expectation and willingness to act, not become frustrated with your friends. That means you need to stop being jealous about the timing in which your friends receive their blessings. Rather than harboring resentment, focus on building your faith and working on your goals.

Like exercise, to build your faith you have to aggressively, persistently, habitually, positively work and sow into your goals so that you can harvest blessings and good experiences of your own. Your unbelief which leads you to waste your time being negative and not accomplishing your life purpose is not your friends fault. Be happy for them, congratulate them, and celebrate with them. Mirror their joy during the moment, and then get back to work on your own life purpose, goals and dreams.

If you are really struggling with your negative emotions, work on your goals and dreams directly before their celebration and as soon as you leave their celebration. Doing so will completely eliminate the time you have available to be envious towards your friends. Create and build reasons of your own to celebrate in the future, but not in a competitive spirit. Simply act each day with purpose and continually reach toward fulfilling *your* life purpose and destiny.

When you feel unrest within yourself, or like you absolutely cannot (or do not) want to be happy for someone when something good happens to them, simply acknowledge that those feelings of unrest, trouble, turmoil, and torture come from a place of fear within you about what you feel you cannot do or may never have for your own life and future. Once you acknowledge and take ownership of your behavior, fix it.

When you feel you can have, experience or at least work toward building a great, exciting future for yourself, you won't have time or energy to hate on or try to sabotage someone else's life or happiness. When negative thoughts and feelings arise within you, pray about them, and start immediately working on building a concrete future for yourself. If you take a positive, productive course of action, the negative feelings will subside.

Be good-hearted and good-natured toward your friends during the good and bad times in their life. Your total life experience will be the better for it. This will require effort, unselfishness and a positive spirit about what is possible for you. However, it is not impossible. Build or get something in your own life to celebrate so that you are not miserable when other people are happy and filled with joy. Everyone experiences rainy days in life, but your perception of your circumstances and your future course of action are your responsibility.

Celebrating milestones and achievements

Celebration is one of the most powerful ways you can nurture your relationships. When you celebrate with someone, throw a bash for someone, or pause your life in some way to show your friends that you are truly happy for them; it simply makes them feel good. Those good feelings you help produce in others will cause them to appreciate your presence in their life and strengthen your relationship. It also provides you with great moments to look back on as your friendship ages.

There are many ways to celebrate your friends. You can start by simply saying congratulations (in-person, call, e-mail or text message). If possible, you could purchase or create a gift, or a thoughtful card. The goal is to compliment their growth and highlight good things about them. Tell your friends what you genuinely like, admire, and appreciate about them during these moments. Plan a party or surprise them with a quiet, special dinner. Just do something to acknowledge what has just occurred in their life.

You must understand the changes and seasons that friends and friendships go through, and celebrate them instead of fear or resist them. Your friends are in the process of achieving their goals and walking out their life purpose. Progress for them is good. When you get scared or maybe feel hurt or resentment because of their progress, take some time to examine your own life and what you currently have or possess that can help you to achieve your own desires and goals. Something within you or around you (a gift, skill, talent, or resource) exists right now in your life that can move you closer to what you desire for your future. Figure out what that is and use it.

You are the only one who can be you and who can fulfill *your* life purpose. If others try to imitate you, view it as a compliment and keep it moving. They will never truly be fulfilled until they give up on trying to be you and step into their own shoes to fulfill their own destiny. If you are the one trying to mimic someone else to get what they have or be who they are - stop it. Trying to obtain what your friend possesses will ultimately frustrate you and quickly destroy your relationship.

Nobody can be you, and you cannot be anyone else.

THOU SHALT CELEBRATE ACHIEVEMENTS

What God has for you, is for you. He has given you your own life purpose to fulfill and has great plans in store for your life. You are not in competition with your friends or anyone else, so you can relax and feel free to celebrate one another and your accomplishments, then continue to pursue God's plan and purpose for you.

Always contact and reach out to your friends when something great is happening in their lives. Send a friendly message when something positive is occurring in their life. At the same time, don't be petty about a friend forgetting or missing one event or day in your life. Consider their life circumstances and what they may be going through before you jump to conclusions or run off on a tangent (in your head or verbally) about what they should've or could've done. Remember, it is nice and a wonderful blessing for others to love and celebrate with you, but life is not all about you.

One important lesson concerning this commandment is to be sure you are there for your friends during the more difficult seasons of their lives to ensure you will not be considered an outsider during their seasons of celebration and progress. Be there for them when they have nothing (because you genuinely love and care about them), so that they will desire your presence when the tide turns and great things happen in their life.

Take some time to figure out today how you can celebrate the life and accomplishments of each of your friends. Celebrate and have fun!! Life is too short not to take advantage of every opportunity to do so. Days of celebration are great ways to engage in fun, invigorating, adventurous activities together to make amazing memories and build or strengthen your friendship.

The real test of friendship is: can you literally do

The 10 Commandments Of Friendship

nothing with the other person? Can you enjoy those moments of life that are utterly simple?
~Eugene Kennedy

What if I have limited resources?

According to Eugene Kennedy, "The real test of friendship is: can you literally do nothing with the other person? Can you enjoy those moments of life that are utterly simple?" That is so very true. It is nice when you are able to do activities and purchase gifts to celebrate with your friends. However in a true friendship it will be your presence, not your presents, that is most appreciated and remembered. So try to celebrate one another somehow, even if it just means spending time with one another. Be creative and use one of your God-given gifts or talents to bless the life of your friend. If you have nothing else to celebrate, get together and simply commemorate your friendship, your willingness to travel through life together, and what you two have contributed to one another's lives. The time and effort you dedicate to your friendships will make all the difference in the quality of those friendships and your life. When your life comes to an end, it will be the time you spent together that matters.

30 Ideas for how to celebrate achievements:
1. Simply pause to say congratulations and how proud and happy you are for your friend.
2. Send a gift and/or card to celebrate a special day in their life, or just to express your appreciation for their presence in your life.
3. Purchase tickets to their favorite sporting event, concert or activity.
4. Take a class together such as a dancing class, the

latest fitness craze, a specialty cooking course, an art/pottery class or a home improvement class (usually offered free at the local hardware store).
5. Put together a DVD filled with video clips, photos, and/or music that reminds you of great times together or important moments in their life. Or keep a scrapbook of your adventures, trips, and times together and present it to them.
6. Send them a gag gift or something to make them laugh just to brighten up their day.
7. Participate in an intramural activity or adult league together (flag football, soccer, basketball, bowling, softball).
8. Throw a special occasion party for your friend (bridal shower, baby shower, birthday, graduation, homecoming, promotion, retirement, anniversary, housewarming) and invite *their* family and other close friends.
9. Plan a nice day outdoors (beach, lake, park) and arrange a picnic or tailgate. Purchase lawn games or a recreational sports bundle from your local superstore for entertainment.
10. If your lives permit, plan a trip or a sleep over, have fun, and act like big kids again.
11. Have a movie night at your favorite theatre, or create your own experience. Purchase inexpensive box candy and popcorn, rent your favorite movie or new release, and just hang out.
12. Get together for physical activity such as working out together, playing sports, bike riding or taking a long walk.
13. Have a theme party (movie theme, western theme, decade theme, collegiate or pro team, luau/hula party, Mexican fiesta, ugly sweater party, scaven-

ger party, karaoke).
14. Prepare a nice home-cooked dinner or host a simple potluck on your friend's behalf. Make or purchase (depending on your culinary skills) their favorite dish or dessert.
15. Plan a spa day of pampering, golfing, fishing, or other relaxing activity.
16. Develop a new interest, activity or hobby together, or rediscover an old one that you two can share .
17. Give your friend a gift card to their favorite activity or store.
18. Have a photo shoot done together. Be creative.
19. Consider trying a new restaurant or exotic food neither of you would usually choose. It will provide you with a conversation piece as well as create a new memory to add to your friendship.
20. Plan a cruise or trip abroad.
21. If you live far apart from one another, plan to meet somewhere each year or every couple of years to reconnect in person.
22. Get together at your friend's favorite coffee house, juice shop, or ice cream parlor.
23. Participate in a boot camp or plan activities that will help you both improve your health and fitness.
24. Have a guys or girls night out filled with activities your friends enjoy or do something new that one or both of you have never experienced before.
25. Have a day out where you let your friend choose exactly what *they* want to do. Be open to a new experience with them if it is something you have never tried before.

Thou shalt celebrate achievements

26. Have your friend's favorite restaurant food, dessert or snack shipped to their house to surprise them (Side note to some of our friends: we are still waiting on our Grippos!)
27. Plan a game night filled with your favorite board, card, or video games.
28. Consider an adventurous day together doing something to heighten the senses such as skydiving, camping, hiking, hot-air balloon rides, white water rafting, or scuba diving.
29. Plan to participate in volunteer work together. Teaming up to help others could prove to be one of the most rewarding activities of them all in building and strengthening your friendship.
30. Create a container or jar of ideas to do or complete together and then randomly draw or pick them out from the container throughout the year to rebuild or strengthen the bond between you.

In order to celebrate your friends, you do not have to perform every item on this list. The 30 suggestions are merely provided as a means to spark ideas and inspire you to be creative within your friendship. If you attempt to put a few of these ideas together, you may be able to recharge your friendship and create a foundation to move forward toward a long-lasting relationship.

Friendship isn't a big thing - it's a million little things.
~Author Unknown

The 10 Commandments Of Friendship

Questions:
- What fears are preventing you from celebrating the life, accomplishments and good experiences of your friend? What steps can you take to restore your faith to become a more supportive friend?
- Make a list of all your friends. How you can do better at celebrating the good things, events, important dates, and activities in their lives?
- Is your calendar updated with all the important days/dates of your friends' lives (birthdays, anniversaries, graduations, holidays, dates of promotion, etc.)?

Commandment III
Thou shalt not exploit kindness

Commandment III - Thou shalt not exploit kindness

Before borrowing money from a friend, decide which you need most.
~American Proverb

Given a healthy home situation, most children tend to view the world through an untainted lens. We constantly marvel at our younger children's perception of the world and how pure their questions and thoughts are. There are some adults who have had this same youthful expectation toward people; assuming others will behave accordingly only to get their feelings hurt in the end.

Unfortunately the most optimistic person still has to deal with difficult people on a daily basis. It is unfortunate that we don't live in a world where kind, purehearted traits are always reverenced. While there are some people that display these characteristics, they are at times few and far between. Genuine kindness, respect, and consideration can be challenging to find.

Similar to the assertion that chivalry is dead, true kindness is rare. The state of being kind is so scarce in fact that there are awards given to those who display unusual, random acts of kindness. It is an inherit trait and ability which we can all possess, however most people chose to ignore it as they become absorbed in self-interests and personal gratification. Therefore, when people are kind towards you, understand it is a gift which shouldn't be taken lightly.

Kindness is very important in social interactions. It is the building block of human relationships which can impact people's lives for years to come. You will always remember two types of people in life; those who are cruel and disruptive to your life, and those who display acts of kindness and love. People who are kind to you leave a lasting, positive impression because it is rare, and you remember their selfless demeanor for years to come as you revere their generosity and compassion towards you.

Being kind, by definition is a very unselfish act. It is giving of yourself, your energy, your time, and your resources. Someone is sacrificing something in order to be a blessing to your life. Therefore as decent human beings, whether it is someone you meet for the first time, a sibling, or friend you've know your entire life; we should never exploit the kindness of others. This should be common knowledge, but oftentimes people are not considerate and have no idea they are taking someone's kindness for granted.

Kindness is usually displayed in three ways; in tangible form (e.g. a gift), through actions, or with time.

Tangible form...
You should be considerate of others instead of attempting to seize possessions or material objects from them. This could apply to assuming occupancy in space that was not given or offered to you, money, or objects that belong to your friends. What they possess is for them to freely give, not for you to feel you have the right to take. Do not try to pressure others to get what you want out of them. That is not characteristic of a friend. Let them give what they desire to give and then you appreciate what you receive.

Furthermore, when someone gives something to you, this is not an invitation to be unappreciative and ask, ask, and ask again for more. I recall one Christmas we gave an extended family member a present only to receive the response, "Do you know you only gave me one gift?" The problem with having this type of ungrateful mind-set and demeanor toward others is that everyone has a breaking point. When you are unappreciative, eventually you will repel people away from you. It will make others you encounter throughout your life not want to give to you at all, or spend time and be around you again. Selfishness and ungratefulness will eventually lead to isolation.

Actions…

When someone gives you an inch, don't take a mile. Appreciate the kind act for what it is and do not take advantage of their generosity. Remember, no one is obligated to do anything for you. The sooner you realize this, the sooner you can build, salvage, and repair relationships in your life.

Similarly, when you are the one extending the act of kindness, offer your generosity without expecting anything in return. Do not throw a temper tantrum when their response doesn't meet your expectations. If you have feelings of anger or resentment at their response, or lack thereof, it is an indicator that you gave with the wrong intentions.

Make sure you are honest with yourself. If the act was truly selfless, you would treat them the same before and after the act of kindness. In life when you selflessly sow into the lives of others, you can expect a harvest in return. However, that spiritual law does not specify what you will receive, when you will receive it, or how you will receive it. In other words, what you reap may not be in the timing or manner you anticipate.

Prematurely and immaturely throwing a temper tantrum about not getting what you want out of someone after doing an act of kindness could lead to you blocking future blessings. Your behavior will cause your reputation to precede you, and others will view your kind acts as false and conditional. Therefore, do acts of kindness selflessly and then live your everyday life pursuing your goals and purpose. When you conduct yourself in this manner, the seeds of goodness you planted in the world will turn into a beautiful, bountiful harvest.

Time…

A similar trait all true friendships share is the allocation of time for one another. This can be challenging at times as individuals grow and life circumstances change the dynamics of a friendship. When this happens, friends find the time they spend together sparse, and sometimes one friend may have a harder time dealing with the distance.

It is understandable to want to be around someone you care about, however try to be cognizant of their time. Good friends are not overbearing or clingy. If you overwhelm your friends by showing up unannounced at all hours, expecting them to be available just because you have free time, or attempt to be around them twenty-four hours a day, they will eventually get fed up with your presence in their life and begin to back away, or literally *run* away from you.

Time applies to the personal space of your friends. When visiting a friend don't stay beyond your welcome. If you receive several hints, verbal and non-verbal (such as putting the kids in bed, yawning, mentioning they have to wake early in the morning, or literally falling asleep while you are talking), then don't ignore those signs or play dumb. Even if you are having the time of your life, wearing out your welcome is one of the surest ways to make certain that your friends will stop calling and inviting you over. Time is valuable, so try to be considerate.

Spending time with one another is great, but hindering your friends from getting rest or having time to allocate toward their life purpose, dreams and goals will eventually become a problem.

The key to considerately spending time is moderation. Time is one of the greatest gifts you can give someone, but you must learn when enough if enough. You will never lose a good friend by being considerate and respectful of their time. Try not to get frustrated with a rough day or possibly a busy season of your friend's life when they may not have as much time available. Be patient and give them space to handle their life so they can make more time for you again in the future.

Time also applies to gifts. When someone gives you a gift, try to think about the impact the gift had on their time and resources. What you may give little value to may be all they have to give to you. You may have no clue how their selfless act affected them personally. Understand that even if your friend is financially prosperous, they are not obligated to do anything for you. Everything you receive from other people, without an exchange for a service or a material object, is a gift. Treat it as such, and let your friends know you appreciate whatever it is they have done.

Always show gratitude for what other people contribute to your life. However, be cautious as there is a thin line between gratitude and guilt. Do not create unnecessary burdens on yourself as you accept the kindness of others. When someone does something for you, it does not mean that you are indebted to them forever; and vice versa. But at least, at the bare minimum, genuinely say thank you and sincerely acknowledge that someone took the time to do something for you.

No matter what the dynamic of your relationship

is, whether you are a friend, spouse, sibling or peer, no circumstance warrants you holding what you have done for someone over their head. You should never at any point in life pull out a checklist and ramble off what you have done for someone because you should have done it freely out of the goodness of your heart. If this is not the case and you have ulterior motives, then you shouldn't have done it at all.

It can be frustrating if someone does not demonstrate appreciation for what you have done for them. But in every situation, you must understand that God sees all that you have done. He knows your heart and the good you have put out into the world, and you can trust it will come back to you or your family in some other way.

If it continues to bother you because you are not getting the appreciation or return you desire, stop doing whatever you are doing. Those feelings that you are having may be because you have been doing those actions with the wrong intentions. When you can come to the point where you are honest with yourself and your friend about what you want out of the situation, then resume the actions when your intentions and desires are clear and have been communicated.

Don't ever take your friends for granted and assume that they have to be a part of your life. If you do, you may ensure that they disappear from your life at some point in the future. Keep it simple; give to others and show your appreciation for what others give to you. Whenever you have an opportunity in the future return the kindness someone has bestowed upon you, stop and return the blessing. Simply be thoughtful and considerate about what is going on in the lives of your friends and sow into their lives when you can. It will improve your life and friendships immensely!

The only way to have a friend is to be one.
~Ralph Waldo Emerson

Questions:
- Have you taken advantage of or been unappreciative of the kindness of others?
- Who do you need to say thank you or show your appreciation to?
- What can you do to show your gratitude and appreciation for their presence in your life?
- Make a list of your friends and family members with a list of kind acts of appreciation you can do for each of them, and then take action. You never know when it will be your last opportunity to do so.

Commandment IV
Thou shalt be truthful

Commandment IV - Thou shalt be truthful

A friend accepts us as we are yet helps us to be what we should.
~Author Unknown

Being truthful and honest (with a spirit of love) can be one of the most challenging responsibilities in a relationship. You have to find a balance between loving and accepting others, and speaking up when you know it is necessary. Taking the feelings of others into consideration before you speak is extremely important. It does not mean that you should not say what needs to be expressed, rather you should think before you speak and attempt to say it in the most loving way possible. Be sensitive to their feelings and what may be going on in their life at the time.

In relationships, people are often dishonest or hide their true feelings out of fear. Fear comes in various forms. Some may fear conflict, being lashed out at, or the punishment that may occur as a result of speaking up. Others fear the silent treatment or feel that they may lose the relationship altogether if they speak their feelings. Regardless of the situation the cost of being silent, holding in your emotions, and letting feelings of resentment fester can be far worse than actually mustering up the strength to tell the truth.

It is more likely that harboring your feelings or lying will cause more damage to your relationship than honesty will. If the truth causes your relationship to end, then it is best to let it go. What good is a relationship if you are unable to express your true feelings? How is it possible to be comfortable or have your needs met in a relationship if you aren't authentic in that relationship?

How is that helpful to your mind, physical health, emotional state and spirit?

If your friend wants you to remain silent or continually appease them so that they never have to face the truth, then you need to reevaluate what type friendship you have. If they are not willing to take anyone else's feelings into consideration, what type of friend is that? You should not have to pretend that nothing is wrong with you, with them, or with the relationship, *when something actually is wrong*, just to keep them in your life. You can never repair what you are not willing to express is a problem to begin with.

Similarly, if you dish it you better be able to take it. If you want others to be able to handle the truth, you need to be able to handle the truth about yourself as well. The same way you feel you should be able to express your honest thoughts and opinions, your friends should be able to reciprocate.

A home built on a bad foundation can lead to a plethora of problems from doors being unable to shut and latch to cracks in the floors and ceilings. These problems start small and can lead to huge problems later on. If the foundation of your friendship was not built on honesty and you chose to not speak the truth, those small cracks can grow until you have a problem that may be irreparable. Further, you cannot ignore the cracks and hold your friend accountable for fixing an issue they were never made aware of.

If you find yourself in a friendship where you are not being 100 percent honest, the first step in repairing your foundation is to tell your friend that you have been dishonest or harboring feelings. It also is a good idea to apologize for not being honest or feeling strong enough to tell them. Let them know why you may have been afraid to share the thoughts, feelings, or information before, and then let it flow from your heart in the most kind, thoughtful way that you can. Whatever the issue may be, pray about it, think it through, and then search for a solution together.

Honesty is refreshing and allows you to be yourself within a relationship. According to Ralph Waldo Emerson, "A friend is a person with whom I may be sincere. Before him, I may think aloud." If you do not have this option in your friendship, what do you really have?

A friend is a person with whom I may be sincere. Before him, I may think aloud.
~Ralph Waldo Emerson

Being able to be truthful, forthright, sincere, frank, candid, direct, and steadfast as a person is of utmost importance in building a real and lasting relationship. Your friends should know that you are going to habitually tell them the truth; and your friends will appreciate the honest thoughts and opinions you share with them in a spirit of love and genuine concern. If your actions are causing you to lie or conceal the truth, then you should probably stop doing whatever that hurtful action is in order to prevent further damage to your friendship.

Don't give room, time and opportunity for resentment to build up in your relationship. If you are truthful, real and genuine, it affords you the opportunity to put all issues on the table and find a mutual solution. If you can't find a solution you both can live with, you can both agree to disagree, or agree to part ways. Either way you will be able to move forward with your life with a sense of peace rather than festering resentment. You won't have to worry about an issue arising or exploding later because you were real and honest with the people you love and care about in your life to begin with.

You should welcome a good friend telling you the truth as they have your best interest at heart. A genuine friend will lovingly tell you the truth about your faults, harmful behavior, destructive habits or people in your life. They will also attempt to help you find a solution that will enable you to grow as a person. This type of friendship is invaluable. Many people will only pacify you to get what they want or can get out of you, but true friends will have those necessary, possibly uncomfortable conversations with you. Frances Ward Weller writes, "A friend can tell you things you don't want to tell yourself." Just because you do not want to hear something, does not mean that it does not need to be said. In many cases it can improve your life, health, and well-being.

A friend can tell you things you don't want to tell yourself.
~Frances Ward Weller

When you address your friend with honesty, this does not mean you have free reign to be disrespectful and hurtful. Life can be stressful at times and individuals face too many challenging situations to feel you can talk reckless to people. Your words very well may be the last thing that makes them snap and go over the edge. So think before you speak, be tactful, try not to be verbally abusive, and don't dish out what you cannot take.

Remember once you put words out into the atmosphere, you can't take them back. Speaking hurtful words to a friend is like throwing a brick through glass window, watching it shatter and then expecting your friend to glue the shards back together again. The window will never be the same, neither will your friendship. Make sure what you are about to say is helpful and spoken with extremely positive sentiments and intentions.

If you desire for your friendships to be strong and long-lasting, don't assume people can read your mind. If you have a problem or issue, address it directly to that person, and not behind their back. We've seen people of all ages sit and pout, throwing monstrous tantrums about an issue no one had a clue they were upset about.

We had an older friend of the family (who definitely should know better) that was mad because no one would acknowledge her tantrum. After months passed, we eventually discovered her tantrum emanated from hurt feelings over a pie. Yes you heard right, a pie. This fully physically healthy person allowed selfishness to dismiss the health of an ailing family member (as if this person wasn't going through enough) and ignored them for months and months over a strawberry pie recipe.

Ultimately if we add common sense to our knowledge of human behavior, we know those issues stemmed deeper than just a pie recipe. But the point is we sometimes let petty situations get in the way of relationships because we aren't man or woman enough to say what we truly feel. So in remembrance of the strawberry pie incident, pause and engage in some time of self-reflection. If there is a person you are upset with and you are ignoring for a petty reason (masking a deeper issue), be grown up about it, put the book down and go talk to them.

Life is too short to be simple, and the worst thing you can do is let a person leave this earth when there are petty unresolved issues on the table. If you find it difficult to speak and articulate your point, write your thoughts, feelings, and opinions in a loving letter. The important thing is that you give them space, room, silence and opportunity to respond on their own timing. If they don't respond, or don't respond how you want them to, it is okay. You are in control of you and you alone.

Be at peace with your own maturity and ability to exercise wisdom and kindly express what you need to communicate. Assess the situation (after you have given it substantial time) and then simply make a decision for what you need to do for your own life. Forgive if the situation requires forgiveness in order for you to heal, and then move on. A true friend will respect your effort and care about your feelings.

If you have done something to really damage the mind, body, possessions, or spirit of a friend, they may not be able to forgive and move forward immediately at this moment in a friendship with you. But they will remember that you took time to sincerely apologize, and you two may be able to repair and rebuild your relationship sometime in the future. Before you speak to your friend, choose your words carefully and delicately wrap the negative issues that need to be addressed in love, admiration, and respect for the good things about your friend. When sharing your feelings, focus on being as gentle and helpful as possible. Your goal should be in their best interest, not just what you want.

Fully understand that you are no more perfect than the friend you are explaining your thoughts, feelings, and opinions to, so be willing to hear their rebuttal. Give them space and a platform to express their feelings. You are the one who was brave enough to bring up the situation, so you are more than likely someone who is mature enough to receive what they have to say.

Keep in mind that your honest opinions or feelings may somewhat blind-side the friend to whom you need to express yourself. They may not have the time to comprehend, think through the issue, and carefully chose their words. As a defense mechanism many people will lash out, so be prepared to accept their response with love. If they string together a series of words which would make Richard Pryor proud and you find yourself becoming angry, take some time to breathe and come back to the issue when you both have a more rational and calm temperament. True friendships will weather these storms.

There is usually some type of risk involved when you decide to express the truth. However, consider what you would lose by not saying anything. You can choose to lie or be quiet and hold your true feelings inside. But what you feel, think, and believe will more than likely surface one way or another. Better to be able to clearly think through what needs to be said and how you would like to express it, than to have it uncontrollably burst out one day in your attempt to hold it all inside.

Honesty leads to your words and opinions having value and worth to your friends. They will label you as the friend whose words are genuine, and know that you are willing to be up front and direct with them 100% of the time. There are many people who like to hear what they want to hear, but you will never truly gain their respect. In life, you receive more respect by being genuine and people knowing they can come to you to obtain total honesty.

You can accept sincere, factual statements from your real friends because you know they love you and have your best interest at heart. If you see your friend going the wrong way, endangering their life, or causing damage to your relationship, then speak up. If your friend responds negatively, forgive him or her, give them room to calm down, and keep it moving. This is a fork in the road for your friendship where things could go left or right.

The 10 Commandments Of Friendship

If your relationship can resume after you both are calm, then that is great. If not, then it is likely some time apart is needed or the relationshp should possibly be severed. In either case if you expressed yourself out of genuine love, care and concern for their well-being, you should not live with any regrets. Both roads will lead to more happiness than if you sat and allowed your friend to self-destruct without saying anything at all.

Check in with yourself to make sure that you are being genuine and authentic in your relationships so that you are not harboring resentment or living a lie. To do that, you must understand what truthfulness and honesty are, and are not. When you are truthful and honest you do not tell little white lies or make misleading statements, you are not counterfeit or have fraudulent hurtful intentions, and you do not alter and tamper with information for your own selfish gain. If any of these behaviors apply to you or how you are conducting yourself, you are doing so because you are fearful about something in your life. Long-lasting friendships require living by faith rather than fear.

Do everything you can in life to refrain from being a coward, yielding to fear, or needlessly destroying your friendships. Say what you mean and mean what you say. Have faith that if you are acting and speaking out of genuine agape love for your friend that everything will turn out how it is supposed to and the situation (all things considered) will work together for your good. Transparency is a welcome trait in true friendships, so do your best to be your authentic self. Be honest with your friends about your feelings. Forthright, sincere, reliable people are challenging to find these days. Love those around you who are, and let them know you appreciate their presence in your life!

If it's very painful for you to criticize your friends - you're safe in doing it. But if you take the slightest pleasure in it, that's the time to hold your tongue.
~Alice Duer Miller

Questions:
- Who have you not been honest and truthful with?
- How would you feel if you were on the receiving end of what you are being dishonest about? How would you feel if that same truth were withheld from you?
- What do you need to be honest and truthful about?
- What is the most kind, loving, thoughtful, gentle way that you can express what needs to be said?

Commandment V
Thou shalt express empathy

Commandment V- Thou shalt express empathy

To have a good friend is one of the highest delights of life; to be a good friend is one of the noblest and most difficult undertakings.
~Anonymous

Empathy is the act of identifying and understanding the feelings, thoughts and actions of others. It is basically placing yourself in someone else's shoes and expressing sincere concern for their situation. In contrast, narcissism is the natural enemy of empathy. It is selfish behavior rooted in "me" love. It is self-gratifying and an unattractive trait within friendships.

How do you know if you have been expressing "me" love versus empathy towards your friends? You may be selfish if you…

- Are always thinking about, talking about, and wanting everyone in your world to focus on and solve your problems versus listening to the issues of others and reciprocating effort in solving their dilemmas.
- Rarely, if ever, stop talking long enough to ask how someone else is doing *and* be quiet long enough after you ask for them to actually answer.
- Call other people, talk for hours straight, and then hang up the phone without the other person having an opportunity to tell you anything about their life.
- Don't know anything about the lives of your friends because you never ask.
- Cannot remember right now when the last time was that you asked about how anyone else was

doing, or cannot remember what the person's response was who you asked.

If your find your behavior on the list above, then this section of the book is dedicated to you on behalf of your friends, family, coworkers, and other people around you that you are most likely driving insane. In order to sustain relationships, you must control this behavior. To control or defeat a thing, you must first understand it.

Narcissism is rooted in selfishness, which is ultimately destructive to all relationships. If you are the sole subject of your thoughts or consciousness, all or most of the time, you may be narcissistic. This behavior is likely problematic not only to your friendships, but to every relationship you ever attempt to have. If your focus is on pleasing yourself verses what is happening in the lives of the people around you, your way of thinking will prohibit you from experiencing true, positive, lasting friendships as your thoughts precede your actions.

It is impossible to be a good friend if you lack consideration for others and are only concerned with your own interest, comfort, and how you feel. If you always disregard the welfare or wishes of others around you in order to get what you want, people will start to avoid you. Further, it is likely they will tell other people about your behavior so they can avoid you too.

You should have some idea of what your friends need or desire for their lives. Why? Because you have asked about what is going on in their life and how they feel. It sounds simple, but try it. You may be surprised at the reactions of the people in your life. You don't have to always be self-serving, tending to only be concerned about advancing your own interest. When you are genuinely concerned about what is going on in the life of your friends, it opens the line of communication. You may learn something new about your friend…or even yourself.

If you have been a self-serving individual the majority of your life and attempt to now express empathy, the initial reaction you may receive from your friends may not be favorable. They may be apprehensive with a facial expression that non verbally states, "What do you want now?" Understand their reaction stems from you constantly wanting something from them, and they may not believe that you have now chosen to morph into a selfless, giving, loving, caring individual overnight. Therefore be prepared and give them time to get used to this new version of you. If you keep pursuing and continue developing the character traits and qualities of being a good friend, eventually their memories of you being a selfish, narcissistic individual will begin to fade in light of the new you.

Stepping outside of yourself does not require hours of your time or an abundant amount of energy. You can let someone know that you care about them through a brief call or e-mail. When they respond about what is happening in their life, your first thought should NOT be, *"How does what is happening in their life directly affect me or prohibit me from getting what I want for my own life?"* Once your friend responds about their current circumstances, take time to think about how their issues or circumstances are affecting *their* life, health, emotional state, and well-being. If you really want to stretch yourself, you could possibly even get creative and come up with a solution or an idea about what you can do to help them. You may not be able to solve their problem, but you could certainly come up with some way to demonstrate that you care or possibly even generate a way to take their mind off of their dilemma for a brief time.

The 10 Commandments Of Friendship

When your idea involves spending time with your friend or wanting your friend to do something for you, just pause and consider what is happening in their life at the moment. If you feel disappointed about their response to your proposal about going out, having them over, or participating in an activity, just consider that them not being able or up to doing what you want may not have *anything* to do with you. Your friends have their own set of problems independent of you. In many cases, they have additional issues on top of their dilemma they have (or may not have) revealed to you that they must also take into consideration. Or they may simply be trying to have one day of peace and alone time in their own hectic day-to-day lives.

Sometimes being a good friend means understanding when your friend needs a little breathing room. If everything does not happen when you want, how you want, on your timing, at your place, your home or your desired destination, it is perfectly okay. This doesn't diminish your friendship in any way. There may be a time in your friend's life in the near future that will be less chaotic that will then grant you two the opportunity to do whatever your idea or desire is. Be patient.

It is fine for you to put your ideas, feelings, and requests out into the world, it is great to want to spend some time with your friends, and it is healthy to be honest and let people know what you want. But, if they do not give it to you or are not able to do what you want, it will still be okay. Whatever is supposed to happen, will happen. What God has for you, is for you. His plans for you and your friends are good, and His timing is perfect. The sooner you realize that, the easier it will be for you to breathe, calm down, and have peace in the midst of whatever is going on around you.

Thou shalt express empathy

Be there for your friend in whatever capacity they need for their situation. Give them space and time to work out whatever is going on in their life if that is what they express to you that they need in the moment. Relax, relate, release. If they need downtime let the issue go, regroup, and try to plan something else at a better time for both of you in the future.

Your friends will always appreciate your understanding far more than your attempts to pressure them for self-gain. Being an understanding friend that expresses empathy is relatively easy. First, look to see what other's needs are and pay attention to their feelings and emotional state. Next, pause to put yourself in their shoes and think. Finally, speak and react after you have fully assessed the situation with consideration for someone outside of yourself.

If you want to be a genuine friend, stop every now and then and sincerely ask how someone else is doing. Don't always pray for and be concerned about your own needs, wants, and desires. Step outside of yourself and go into intercessory prayer for your friends as well. Pray for wisdom, solutions, and see if there is anything that you can do to be of assistance to them.

Please ensure when you offer assistance that it is something that is helpful to *them* not just you. Also make sure that it is something you honestly want to do and that you will not resent them for afterwards. If your heart is not sincere in your attempt to help, then don't bother. Do what you can in their life with love and sincerity, not to build a list for your own ego of what you have done for others.

On the other hand, whenever or if you cannot be there for a friend in the exact way that they would like due to your own life circumstances, your friend should trust your heart and not misinterpret your inability to visit, give something, or be there with them as a personal attack. They should be able to talk to you about any feelings they have about you not being there. They should also be willing to hear the reason or circumstances surrounding your absence.

Friendships require understanding, love, and a willingness to forgive. Both persons in a friendship need to understand the life events, major changes and seasons of their friend's life. To have a great friendship you both must accept one another's seasons of growth. Changes in geographic location, residence, career, education, financial status, economic shifts, relationship status or marriage, having children, a family crisis and health issues are all types of personal life changes that will require some adjustments in the friendship. When these seasons occur, friends must make a conscious choice to proceed with the friendship during these life changes. More than likely you will choose to hold onto the friendship if you are more interested in giving into your friend's life than you are about what you can get out of your friend's life.

We can always refer back to the Golden Rule for how to manage and conduct ourselves in our friendships and relationships. One should treat others as one would like others to treat oneself. That simply means do not expect anything from others that you are not willing to do, be or give yourself. You cannot expect others to sacrifice their time, resources, skills, talents, and ability when you would not be willing to sacrifice the same amount of time, energy, and resources for them.

This commandment is not to instruct you to ignore your own goals, hopes, aspirations and dreams. Empathy was addressed merely to assist you in becoming a more considerate friend to the people you care about in your life. Choosing to step outside of yourself will increase your ability to build friendships and maintain the ones you already have. It will also help you to experience a more fulfilling life than if you dedicate your existence to focusing on yourself, your needs, your wants, your problems, and your desires. Accept the advice lovingly then make the most of your life and the relationships you have been blessed to experience.

Questions:
- When you ask someone how they are doing, do you wait *and* listen for their response?
- How can you step outside of yourself today?
- Who can you show genuine love, care, and concern for today?
- Who can you call, e-mail, text or message to check on right now?
- Whose need, want or desire can you make happen for them today?
- What kindness can you bestow upon each of your friends and family members today, without expecting anything back from them in return?
- Who can you pray for who may need it today?

Commandment VI
Thou shalt not be controlling

Commandment VI - Thou shalt not be controlling

A true friend never gets in your way unless you happen to be going down.
~Arnold H. Glasow

There are some events in life that are out of our control regardless of strong will, money, resources, contacts, or power. When these situations occur, one of the most frustrating challenges is managing that feeling of losing control. If you take a second to reflect, I'm sure you can name several circumstances that have been thrown your way that you never thought you would or should have to tackle.

Some individuals discover ways to overcome and move beyond these obstacles. Others live daily with regrets from previous life choices; oftentimes dreaming of how their life would have been different *if they had only*. Once they return to the reality of their circumstance, feelings rise to the surface such as guilt, anger, resentment, anxiety, bitterness and jealously. These emotions make people act in irrational ways, and all stem from the inability to control their current situation.

Controlling personality types all have one common denominator – there is an area in their life where they have lost control and they are having a hard time dealing with it. The need to control other people is a behavior birthed out of fear for what may happen in your own life. Fear of not getting what you desire, fear of being unloved or unvalued, fear of being left out if other people become friends or connect in anyway, fear of missing out on an event or opportunity, fear of financial lack, fear of your needs not being met in a relationship, and/or fear of the actions of others hurting you.

We all have fears we must overcome. If left unaddressed, fears can become obstacles to building a powerful personal faith. With increased faith, you will no longer allow fear to evoke negative thoughts and emotions. It will bless your relationships as the absence of fear allows for the development of a positive outlook on life.

Figure out what your fears are and do what is necessary to confront them. If you need to consult with or hire a professional, then do so. You will need power, love, and a sound mind to take the course of action necessary to conquer your fears. Be determined to learn how to possess all three and put them into action. Don't allow your fears to prohibit or keep you from positively connecting with others throughout your life journey. Life is too short and too precious to miss out on the most important and valuable part of it - positive relationships.

Characteristics of controlling people

What are some characteristics and behaviors of a controlling person? Controlling people are usually self-centered. They will attempt to make you rearrange your schedule to fit their desires without any regard to your inconvenience. Controlling personalities usually find great pleasure in dominating others, using guilt to pressure others into obligatory duties. They attempt to use their position or role in your life to gain control over you, your time, your energy, your skills and your resources instead of allowing you to freely give when you are ready, willing, and able. They also use temper tantrums, abusive behavior, and/or manipulation to get their way.

Controlling people tend to gravitate toward people in a bind, special circumstance, or with a need. They use various means of manipulation to get their way such as emotional leverage (guilt), financial leverage, and other resources. Life with a controlling person is peachy when you adhere to their every request or demand. Their demeanor is calm, content and they are usually in good spirits if they are getting their way. However the second you decide to stand up for yourself and say "no" (one of the best words in the English dictionary you can learn to prevent others from taking control of your life), they mentally lose it. They may even attempt to sabotage you or other relationships in your life.

Individuals who feel the need to control others tend to isolate people in order to have sole rights to them. In their minds, this allows them to get you to do what they want, when they want, without outside interference. When you befriend others, they view this as a threat and are destructive (e.g. attempting to stir up conflict or trouble).

Controlling individuals tend to act like children. If they don't get their way, they pout and throw tantrums. Some may even literally kick, fall out, throw objects and slam doors (alone and in front of others). These individuals secretly put people on punishment through the silent treatment; vowing that everyone will be sorry if they don't do what they want. In many cases they will just stop speaking to you altogether because they do not know how to manage losing control. Your new friendships or relationships cause them to be reminded of their own insecurities and fears.

If you recognize these actions and you know you have been abusive and controlling to others, then (in a loving but scolding tone) stop it! You need to pause, gain control of your actions and your emotional state, and tell yourself to stop acting like an adolescent. Your level of faith for what is possible for your life needs to grow and expand. Whether it is toward a friend, sibling, co-worker, spouse or family member, if you want to sustain your relationship you need to do whatever is necessary to change this pattern of behavior in your life.

If you choose not to address this behavior, you more than likely will lose everyone around you. Even the people that love you or some who may currently seem to worship the ground you walk on will eventually reach a breaking point. This pattern of losing people in your life will continue until you realize that *you* are the common denominator in these failed friendships.

Caring for someone should be an unconditional act. If you feel the need to throw a tantrum or put someone on punishment for not doing what you want, then you need to carefully assess your behavior. When you care for someone, it means you respect their independence and the fact that they have their own life and will be available or come around on their own timing. If it does not happen when or how you want, it is okay. If you find yourself becoming upset, then more than likely in this situation you are more worried about what you can get out of your friend than what you can give to them. Once again, that is not being a true friend.

If you are concerned about giving or making life better for them, your extended hand, friendship, and/ or gift will always be there – when *they* are ready! Caring for someone means sometimes you need to give your friends time and space to handle their own life. Any unkind actions, silent treatment, speaking negatively behind their back, or destruction of the relationship that you choose to partake in while they manage their life tells more about you, your motives, and your insecurities than it does about them.

Do not attempt to make your friend's life your own, and try not to be an overwhelming person. Coming on too strong or being possessive is a way of trying to control others, and it will eventually if not immediately run them away. Understand that you cannot make people be your friend, force them to have the same priorities or interests at the exact same moment as you, or obligate them into spending time with you. When you make offers or plans, people can accept if they desire to or when they can.

It is important to understand you don't know every detail, challenge, obligation, or trial in the life of your friend, and may not understand even if they attempt to explain it to you. Therefore, you must accept and respect their decisions for their life and stop attempting to punish the world when you don't get your way. Be considerate, empathetic and kind while your friends handle their own lives or you will eventually end up alone.

Allowing distance

Pick your closest friend, and think about some of the most intimate conversations you've had. Even in those conversations, I can guarantee you don't know every thought, worry, insecurity, fear, emotional problem, and health issue of that friend – no matter how close you are. After addressing the principles of Commandment V (empathy), you must realize that your friend may need a break sometimes for their own emotional, physical and spiritual well-being.

Allowing distance should not bring your friendship to an end. However there are some instances where people go through seasons of life where they need that separation. If this happens to be the case, then do not attempt to sabotage their other relationships. Just continue to do what is necessary for your own life and maintain your lane.

THE 10 COMMANDMENTS OF FRIENDSHIP

When someone needs to walk away from the friendship or simply take a breather to work on an issue in their personal life, let them. You two may reconnect and be able to build a stronger relationship at a later time if you let them manage their life and use of their time when necessary. People who respect the space of their friends and allow them to manage their own life are remembered in a positive light. It is almost guaranteed that the friendship will completely dissolve if you do not give a person room to breathe when they need it.

Sometimes you'll find yourself in a situation with a friend who is being unnecessarily critical and is always telling you what you should be doing. There is a difference between telling a friend the truth because you love them and want what is best for their life, and badgering them because of your own insecurities. These are the individuals in life that you have to walk on eggshells around because you never know what harsh, ignorant or foolish words they are going to say next.

Your true friends will encourage you to always grow, stretch and mature to become all that you can be. However in doing so they will speak to you in a loving, not controlling, way. They can share their thoughts in a kind, respectful tone and then step back and allow you to make your own life decisions. If you have a friend that rarely, if ever, encourages you or tells you anything good about yourself, then that has more to do with their own insecurities and failures in life than it does with you.

If you have a person or people in your life like this, it may be time to put some space between the two of you. If their words or actions are abusive to your emotional state, mind, body or spirit, you may have to release that friend altogether. Attempt to discuss the issue with them first as they may not even know that their words or actions have been hurtful to you. If you cannot even approach them to discuss the issue, then that is telling of the state of your friendship and how bad the situation has gotten. That being the case, it may be necessary to separate yourself from that person and work on you until you can muster up the courage to stand up for yourself.

Sometimes it is difficult to address these concerns with a friend due to past issues where others may have previously damaged your self-esteem and confidence. You may need some time away to realize that you are strong enough to stand up for yourself. Therefore remove yourself from the situation so you can regroup and heal. When you become strong, self-confident and bold enough to address the issue with them, you two may be able to re-establish and rebuild your friendship in the future. You have to do what is necessary to live your best life. For now, if your needs, feelings, thoughts and desires are never up for consideration, then they have to go!

How to let go of control?

If you are the type of person who gets frustrated because other people do not feel exactly how you want them to feel, and do exactly what you want them to do, then you need to pause, assess your own life, and consider why you are getting so upset? Why do you feel the need to control other people?

Fear is obviously one issue at the root of your problem, so what is it you are scared of? What are you afraid that you'll miss out on? If your friend does not change their feelings or course of action, how will that affect you and what you want? How will it hinder your blessings and progress in life?

You must take time to pause and be truthful with

The 10 Commandments Of Friendship

yourself. Once you honestly answer these questions, you will have the necessary information to make positive changes in your own life. At this point, you should seriously consider switching your focus off of others and begin to concentrate on the life you have full control over – yours.

What actions can you take to enhance your own life without harming others? How can you gain peace in your life, and allow the need to control others to subside? Breathe, do what *you* can do, and then relax and breathe some more. Trust that when you begin sowing positive actions, words and energy into your own life and the world around you that you will receive positive experiences and opportunities in return.

Whether it is a friend or family member that you feel the need to have control over, you must understand it is not your purpose in life to control anyone else's destiny. You can encourage others, but attempting to control everything about their life will only cause them to eventually rebel and possibly decide to remove you from their life.

Instead, take control of your own life and let other people live theirs. They will end up on the path that they are supposed to be on without you shoving them there. If not, that is okay too because that is their life choice.

A friend is one who knows you and loves you just the same.
~Elbert Hubbard

While navigating your role as a friend, sibling, family member, or co-worker, you may find it difficult to relinquish your perceived power. Regardless of the situation, there are two simple concepts to understand which will alleviate your urge to be a control freak. By meditating on and implementing these concepts, you should be able to develop the type of character which will sustain, encourage and enrich your relationships.

    1. Understand that promotion comes from God (*see* Psalm 75:6-7). If you trust this truth, you will put action with your faith, do all you can do in your life, field of work, and relationships and then be at peace with whatever happens after that. Plant your positive seeds, water them regularly, and trust that they will grow into something beautiful in the correct time and season. Remember, seeds that you plant do not become a full size plant the same day and everything in life does not always happen immediately.

    2. Know that God has amazing, wonderful plans for your life and they will happen when they are supposed to happen. There is an old saying that if you want to hear God laugh, then tell Him your plans. Life does not always happen how we want, but God's ultimate plan for your life will prevail (*see* Proverbs 19:21). His plans are better than any plan you could ever create for yourself. Therefore do the best you can to work toward your goals, plans and dreams, but know that what God has for you is better than what you can hope, think or imagine. Further, the plans He has for others (e.g. your friends) are greater than what you can force them into.

From this point forward, try your best to build, maintain, and heal your relationships. If at any point someone cannot spend time investing into your friendship or your goals, simply give them space. Forcing a person to give you everything you desire for your life, or trying to control what they want (or who they want) is not a way to sustain a lasting friendship. You can however choose to be a good friend and be there when they have time or when they may need you in the future. Focus on working toward fulfilling your life purpose and ambitions. Your friend focusing on their own life should not hinder you from achieving your goals.

When gardening sometimes if you plant seeds too close, what you are attempting to produce will not grow due to the inability to receive nourishment. Sometimes friendships need space so individuals can grow. Therefore sow seeds, but give your relationship time and possibly even space so it can have room to mature.

If you truly care about your friend, you will give them space to grow, handle their life, and flourish. Friendships, like gardening, need cultivating and time. You cannot put your hand into soil and expect or force vegetation to immediately burst out of a seed. Similarly with friendships, your harvest from what you have sown into them and the relationship will occur in due time. Don't sabotage your friendships because they are not growing at the pace you would like. If you can be patient, the end result will be so much better than the current state of your friendship.

The Controlled

What do you do when you are the person or friend being controlled? To deal or cope with a controlling person you have to muster up the courage to stand up for yourself; regardless of the backlash you may receive. If you know you have been allowing someone else to control your life, it is time to take the steering wheel back and regain control of your own time, life, resources and destiny.

People will use you as a doormat if you allow them to. You are the only person in the world who can truly teach other people how to treat you. In some relationships, people may try to test your limits to see how far they can push you, what they can get out of you, and what they can get away with.

You have to learn how to set limits and boundaries in your life, and know them prior to someone pushing the envelope so that you can calmly, confidently tell them "no" when the situation occurs. A firm "no" is much better than allowing a situation to fester until you are pushed too far and it develops into an explosive argument.

How do you know if you are in a relationship with a controlling person? Controlling people are rarely empathetic, and usually ignore your situation and constantly make demands in spite of what you are going through. They also disregard how you feel, and attempt to alter your thoughts, feelings or emotions in an attempt to push their personal agenda. For example, you tell your friend you are tired, hurt, or unhappy and they tell you "No you're not." Your opinions are irrelevant as they are hindering something they want. During times of excitement or enthusiasm, controlling people may attempt to crush your elated emotional state instead of being happy with and for you.

When people attempt to control your life, feelings and emotions, it has absolutely nothing to do with you. They feel the need to exert control over other people to cope with loss of control in their own life. It is one thing to give someone loving, kind advice. There are times where a friend needs to cheer up another, or assist them in viewing their situation with wisdom or in a more positive light. That is completely different from ignoring their emotions altogether, knocking them off their emotional high, or trying to force them to feel a different way.

People can choose to listen and encourage others in their friendships. Or they can choose to be the type of friend who assumes they know how you think and feel, never listen, cut you off whenever you attempt to speak, and never give you the opportunity to express your thoughts, feelings, or emotions.

Let's be clear. You having control of your own life, is not up for argument. It is something that just must be. If an argument ensues because you want control of your own life, shut the conversation down. Completely remove yourself from the situation and refuse to argue or debate about it. The right to control your own destiny already belongs to you. It's your life.

If talking to express your needs and feelings has not gotten your point across to your friend, silence will. If your friend continues to argue with you about it, then understand you are wasting time rationalizing with an irrational individual (who is clearly having an emotional breakdown from losing control). At this point, you should realize that your time is too valuable to spend as a verbal or physical punching bag. Lovingly let them have their emotional breakdown, throw their temper tantrum, and walk away as they lay out on the floor all by themselves.

Adult tantrums are an ugly sight that no one should have to witness. When they calm down, get a reality check, and gain some composure about themselves, maybe you two can talk again. If that never happens, oh well. Don't take it personal. Love them from a distance. Their tantrum is an outward statement regarding their inner state and issues in their own life. You can't make them become a better person or friend. They have to do that on their timing when they are ready. You simply keep your power and control over your own life in silence. Forgive them, let it go, stay positive, keep it moving, and befriend others who will love, encourage, and respect you.

Understand your role
Attempting to control other people may get you what you want for a little while from people who are not strong enough to stand up for themselves, but in the end you will kill and destroy all of your relationships. Everyone has a threshold and eventually people in your world will get tired of you and rebel. Therefore, we encourage you to take this opportunity to choose to be a better person and friend so that you will not be alienated. You should be so busy accomplishing your goals, dreams, and life purpose that all you have time to do is love and encourage other people as they accomplish theirs. Get out of their business and get busy with your own.

If you are a controlling person and are driving the people in your life bananas because you feel you have lost control in your own personal life, then choose to change. It's a choice. Consciously choose another path. Exerting control or authority over the lives of others is not your place. Take control of your own personal life and let your friends and loved ones live theirs.

You can lovingly, respectfully share your thoughts, feelings and opinions with your friends, and then they can make their own choices for their own life. That is all you can or should do. You can then have more time and opportunities to create the life you desire for yourself. In a friendship, understand your role. You are only the boss of you. You can only control what is or is not a part of your life, not what is or is not a part of theirs.

If you have a controlling person or controlling people in your life, discuss with them how you feel about it. Stand up for yourself. Remember that beautiful, empowering word "no" and understand that no one can control you unless you allow it.

You teach others exactly how to treat you. Give them an opportunity to back off, grow, and change. If they refuse to listen and their behavior continues, you may have to politely tell them to kick rocks with open-toed sandals, and love them from a distance (grin). We joke, but seriously sometimes it becomes necessary to remove people from your life so they can go take control of their own. You must do whatever is necessary for you to have peace, tranquility, and joy in your life.

The most beautiful discovery true friends make is that they can grow separately without growing apart.
~Elisabeth Foley

Self-Reflective Questions:
- Who in your life are you trying to control right now through your words, actions, or possible temper tantrums?
- How can you release or relinquish the control of others?
- What in your own life can you focus on doing and achieving so that you are not so consumed with the lives and choices of others?
- What can you do to take control of your own life so that others are not controlling you?
- Who do you need to be honest and firm with about your feelings and the direction of your life?
- Who in your life do you feel you need to walk on eggshells around?
- What is it inside that is preventing you from saying "no" and taking charge of your life, time, resources and destiny?

COMMANDMENT VII
Thou shalt be supportive

Commandment VII - Thou shalt be supportive

If a friend is in trouble, don't annoy him by asking if there is anything you can do. Think up something appropriate and do it.
~Edgar Watson Howe

Humans are designed to be social beings. Through this social interaction we establish trust within relationships and form bonds. At times in life, we may need emotional and spiritual support from these relationships in order to sustain the weight of our life experiences and circumstances. The goal of a good supportive friend is finding the balance between providing for your friend's needs through challenging times in their life without neglecting or losing sight of your own.

Know your limits…

Sometimes it is challenging to give your time and not feel like you are being abused or taken advantage of. The best way to combat that feeling is to make sure your intentions for what you do or give is an unselfish act birthed from your heart, as opposed to what you will get in return. When you freely give of your time, resources, and talents without expecting something in return, resentment toward one another is far less likely to build up and cause destruction in your relationship.

A supportive friend provides emotional stability, advice, and encouragement when it is needed. Figure out what you can do to give to support your friends, but don't make the mistake of offering something you can't afford to give (e.g. time or resources). If you are honest with yourself and others about what you can unreservedly give, then you will eliminate the possibility of harboring resentment towards your friends for losing something you can't retrieve. Only offer what you have and are willing to freely give. Whether physical, material, or emotional, to give freely means you can afford to let it go without going through withdrawal afterwards.

To be a good friend at times may require sacrifice on your end. When you see a friend stuck knee deep in mud, you should go to pull them out without a second thought; even if it means you have to get muddy too. Don't just stand there and gawk or talk about them with others. Do what you can to the best of your ability to assist them.

At the same time, your friend should understand what you are able to give, and not hold you responsible for their repeat offenses. We all know somebody that continues to make the same mistakes (which yield the same results). But at some point in their lives accountability must come into play, and you must realize it is not your job to continue to pull them out of their muddy circumstance.

Whenever you support a friend the best that you can, they will likely never forget it. Moments as such create a stronger bond in friendships, so do all you can for your friends. However, be honest with yourself about what you can and cannot do. Understanding your limitations will prevent you from developing resentment, which may possibly lead to the friendship dissolving.

Spending time…

Sometimes when your friends are going through challenging times, they may simply need your companionship. Allot time to be there for them. The time you spend talking, laughing and possibly crying together- could be therapeutic and be a great blessing to you as well.

THOU SHALT BE SUPPORTIVE

If they need space make sure you give them room and opportunity to sort out things on their own time. Ask your friends what they need and what they would like? Listen to their feelings and what they need in that moment. Try to understand their priorities and what must happen in what order in their life. After you consider these factors and if they are up for it, then try to do something positive to enjoy one another's company.

Spending time could also mean supporting your friends in their endeavors. You achieve this by simply taking time out of your schedule to acknowledge what they are doing or accomplishing. Just take a brief pause to encourage them and say congratulations when the task or goal is complete.

When you are pressing towards your goals and dreams, sometimes people will speak discouraging words into your life. They may even smile, but their actions show that they despise the fact you are working toward a goal, let alone succeeding at accomplishing it. Thus having the support of positive friends along the way makes a world of difference.

This is your opportunity to step up to the plate and be sincerely happy for your friends. Encourage and admonish them in their endeavors. If you can manage to do this consistently in the life of others, you will likely always have friends. Share in the good fortune and good experiences with your friends whenever you have the opportunity to.

It is not so much our friends' help that helps us, as the confidence of their help.
~Epicurus

The 10 Commandments Of Friendship

If there is ever a time when your friend expresses that they need or want you to be somewhere, and you are unable to fulfill their request because of a truly pressing matter or a previous commitment you cannot get out of, don't stress about it. Simply explain the situation to your friend. Be at peace because outside of this incident, you know that you are and have been a good friend. If you are always trying to be the best friend that you can be, they should understand the rare occasions when you may not be able to be with them.

You should also trust that your friendship will survive this one incident if you both care about one another's well-being. Send your apologies and congratulations if you can't be there. If possible do something special together to celebrate the occasion the day prior to or shortly after. Your true friends will understand if your life circumstances or situations make it impossible for you to be where they want, when they want. A true friend will look outside of themselves and trust your heart. A wise person will be okay whether people around them do what they want or not.

Be appreciative…

When you find the rare treasure of friends who are willing to be there and offer their support, kindness, love, help, talents, and resources, don't take advantage of them. Time is an extremely precious commodity, so don't waste the time of others or take their presence for granted.

It is the friends you can call up at 4 a.m. that matter.
~Marlene Dietrich

Thou shalt be supportive

You should be able to call your friends at 4 a.m. in an emergency situation if you need them, but you should not abuse their friendship and call them at 4 a.m. every day. This would seem to be common sense, but for some reason people allow their wants to cloud their judgment towards respecting others time and boundaries. Not respecting, valuing, or appreciating the time that people take out of their life for you is another sure way to lose current and future friends. Once again remember, life is not all about you.

Ten ways you can be supportive of your friends…

1. ***Be patient*** - Give them space when they need it, and then be there for them when and if they are ready.
2. ***Acknowledge them*** - Simply ask, "How are you doing? What's the matter? Is there anything I can do?" to acknowledge they have a need to meet.
3. ***Be empathic*** - Attempt to understand and accept the feelings, condition or state of mind of your friends. This alone can greatly enhance your relationships with everyone you come in contact with. Simply taking the time to care about what is going on in the life of other people around you is revolutionary behavior. Think about what you would like someone to say or do for you if you were in the same situation, and then do it. If they are your true friend, you should know something about them. Whatever you don't know, take this opportunity to ask, listen to, and hear their response.
4. ***Accentuate positives*** - Point out what is positive

about your friend and their life. Acknowledge their good characteristics, attributes, contributions, and accomplishments. Do it in a sincere encouraging way that can help improve their self-esteem. Let them know what you love and value about them, and enable them to place their focus on something more positive than the challenges they may currently be facing (that you may know or may not know about).

5. *Give a gift* – Sometimes it is not the price of the gift, but the thought that counts. If possible, pick up a card or gift to encourage your friend. If your funds or resources are limited, create something special with your God-given talents or ability.

6. *Spend time or give space* - If your friend needs someone to spend time with them, then schedule a friendly visit whenever your schedules allow. However if they need space, give them room to process what has happened in their life, and begin to repair or rebuild.

7. *Be an ear to vent* - Be a listening ear. Sometimes people just need to vent, express their feelings, and talk things through with someone. Many times people find a solution to their own dilemma just from hearing their own words. So take the opportunity to be quiet and attentively listen as they sort their life out. If they ask your opinion, you can interject your thoughts then. Don't use your friend's time of need as an opportunity to talk about yourself and your life. Just be there for them.

8. *Seek counsel* – Some situations may be bigger than your capabilities. Some emotional and physical damage may require your friend to seek

the assistance of licensed professionals. If your friend seems unable to cope with or recover from a situation that has occurred in their life, help them seek out and search for professional help to aid them in getting through it.
9. ***Know your limits*** - Sincerely offer to help in whatever way you are *willing* and able. Don't offer to do something that you are going to resent doing, as that is not helpful to your relationship. Make sure that you check-in with yourself to make sure that you are not being selfish and self-absorbed in what you are not willing to offer.
10. ***Simply be there*** - When everyone else is too busy or turns their back on your friend in life, do what you can do to be there for them. In the words of Aristotle, "The antidote for fifty enemies is one friend." You will have much less regret in life when you choose to be there for your friends verses if you choose not to.

The most I can do for my friend is simply be his friend.
~Henry David Thoreau

Love, take pleasure, interest and delight in your friendship. Be there for your friends whenever you possibly can. Serve, promote the interests of, aid, and provide for the needs of your friends. You can do so comfortably now because you have taken time to exercise wisdom in assessing who your true friends are, and those individuals who are not (refer to the previous sections on good and bad friend characteristics). It is also much easier to be a support system for your friends when you are content and happy with your own life. Keep believing in what is possible for you, and pressing toward your goals and dreams.

Also, be willing to accept the love, care and support of your friends in return. Let someone be there for you when you need it. Doing all of the above will greatly enrich and enhance your life, as well as bring great joy, peace and contentment to your spirit.

Self-Reflective Questions:
- Who in your life right now needs your love, help, and support?
- What can you do right now to give support to your friends and show them that you care?
- Who do you need to thank and express your gratefulness to for the love, support, care, favors, and/or gifts they have given to you?

Commandment VIII
Thou shalt not gossip

Commandment VIII - Thou shalt not gossip

He gossips habitually; he lacks the common wisdom to keep still that deadly enemy of man, his own tongue.
~ Mark Twain

Gossiping is one of the most harmful types of communication. It is indicative of idle time that would be better spent reaching goals and pursuing one's own dreams. It is in most cases malicious talk, there is usually intent to do harm behind it, and the majority of the time it is hurtful and destructive to your relationships with others.

For many people it has just become a way of life and they do not even realize how much time they waste by doing it. The truth is gossiping is never truly beneficial to *anyone* involved; the person being gossiped about or the person doing the gossiping. Yes, it may be entertaining to listen to or engage in gossip, and many websites and talk shows have gained popularity and reaped financial benefits as a result. But it doesn't feel good nor is it the most uplifting experience to be the one being gossiped about.

Just because an opportunity to do something exists, doesn't mean that you should do it or engage in it. It may even feel good to be around someone whose personality is charismatic or funny as they gossip, but it is highly likely that you will become the butt of the jokes and gossip when you are not around. There is an old Irish saying which states "Who gossips with you will gossip of you."

Gossipers...

When you meet someone who regularly engages in idle talk or is chatty about others with a mean-spirit, it should raise a red flag. Even if they are hilarious, charismatic or fun to be around in the moment, it may be wise to stay clear of them. W. Somerset Maugham said, "When you choose your friends, don't be short-changed by choosing personality over character."

You may find yourself laughing or chuckling at the gossip they share about others lives, but the negative parts of their personality and the way you see them treat others will be the same way they are likely to treat you in the future. It is possible that the discussion about someone else and their life is completely true, but it does not mean that you speaking of it and sharing it with others is any less harmful.

The best practice is to avoid speaking negative words towards someone and their situation. This way you ensure that you are conducting yourself in a manner becoming of or deserving of good things to return to you. Carry yourself in a manner and only say the things you would say if the person you are gossiping about was standing in the midst of the conversation with you. Don't sow seeds of negativity that you'll end up reaping later on in your life.

Gossip needn't be false to be evil - there's a lot of truth that shouldn't be passed around.
~Frank A. Clark

Why do people gossip?

Spending your time gossiping is a way of filling a void in your life. People gossip because they aren't happy with their lives, thus they talk about others rather than spending their time fulfilling their life purpose, accomplishing their goals, or doing anything to bless the lives of others. Gossiping is an indicator that you are not using your time as productively as you could. It is birthed out of misery and lack of fulfillment in your own life. Once you start using time towards accomplishing more positive life goals and transforming your own life situation, your contentment will subdue any desires you have to spread harmful information about other people.

Gossip is the opiate of the oppressed.
~Erica Jong

Idle time is the catalyst to most gossiping behavior. This can simply be defined as time where you are not engaging in work related to your life purpose. During these times you will find yourself spending moments in inactivity, feeling discontent or empty, or spending your time wastefully. The inability to effectively, productively use your time can lead to you being unhappy or bitter enough to spend your time gossiping.

Even if you are engaging in gossip with a light-hearted demeanor, a smile, or laughter you are still demonstrating this behavior due to deficiencies in your life. In that moment when you notice yourself engaging in gossip, you need to figure out what those deficiencies are and exert effort toward fixing it.

There was a famous comedian that was interviewed and during the series of personal questions he revealed that a lot of his material emanated from the pain in his life. Gossip is similar as it is an outward expression of internal frustration or pain. This may derive from that person having something you may desire for your own life or due to hurt from a past experience. The key is to acknowledge what the root of this issue is so that you can address it and stop this negative, destructive behavior.

THE 10 COMMANDMENTS OF FRIENDSHIP

How to stop gossiping...

When you feel or hear yourself gossiping, ask yourself:

- Why do I want to harm this individual?
- What am I lacking?
- What am I hurting about?
- What do I fear I will never have or experience?
- Why do I even have time for this behavior?
- How can I better spend my time and use my resources?
- What good things can I do or accomplish in my own life and for others in the world?
- What can I do to work toward and succeed at my own life goals instead?

Answer these questions and make certain that you have dedicated time to discovering what your life purpose is. Once you understand your purpose in life, you'll learn how to restrain from this behavior as you're occupied with your own business. Furthermore, keeping your mouth shut is an unwritten portion of the friendship code. Choosing to be a true, honest friend to someone is similar to taking an oath or being bound by a confidentiality agreement.

Since many people struggle to maintain lasting healthy relationships, let's examine a few pages from this unwritten friendship code. A good friend will not tell their friend's business. A true friend realizes that it is not their place to spread anything spoken in confidence. You should be able to confide in and share secrets and intimate details with your friends without them sharing it with the world. Similarly, they should be able to share details of their life with you without having to worry about you running off at the mouth. You should never say any words about your friends behind their back that you would not say if they were standing in the midst of your conversation to their face.

There is always a way you can get out of gossiping. Simply choose to be quiet. If someone tries to pull you in, advise that it is none of your business to discuss and that you do not want to get involved. Words are influential and always start courses of action. You never know what emotional state someone is in, therefore it is a good idea to always assume someone is fragile or on the edge.

Your tongue is powerful therefore you should always watch what you say, and think before you open your mouth. Your silence or the removal of your physical presence from a moment of others gossiping can cease the behavior. If there is no one on the receiving end of the gossip, the person on the speaking end of the conversation loses all their power.

Preserve your tongue with personal issues as well. It would be nice if we could trust everyone with our innermost thoughts, feelings, and secrets but the truth is that everyone is not trustworthy. For those who are not, decrease the amount of ammunition they have to harm you by being wise in what details of your life you choose to share. Everyone cannot handle knowing personal information about others. Yes, people can randomly make up information or lies about you. But many times, most gossip contains at least a crumb of truth. Choose wisely what you choose to share and who you choose to share it with to limit your own regrets.

The impact…

Spreading gossip damages people and relationships. Don't sow discord, conflict, or strife among others. Do everything you can to contribute to unity. As a friend, you should always be the one coming to the defense of your friends when they are under attack, verses being the attacker. Instead of wasting time gossiping, use your time to speak loving words to and about your friends and those you care about. Encourage them in their goals, endeavors, and life purpose.

Sharing details with one another brings your friendship or relationship closer. Don't mess up the opportunity to grow closer to your friends by running your mouth about things that were supposed to be kept between the two of you. You will damage the trust between you that will be very difficult if not impossible to repair. Don't betray your friend's confidence in you.

If you have done or are doing so right now, what does that say about you? What are you expecting to receive in return in life? If you see a situation where you have betrayed a friend's confidence or you are currently doing something to betray a friend, do what you can to stop it, apologize, resolve, and fix it. You get one chance at life, so stop doing things to sabotage your friendships and relationships with others along your journey.

Think about the impact your words and actions may have on others. Protectively care for, be faithful to, and display some type of devotion to the people you care about through your words and actions. If you don't feel strong enough at the moment, at the very least simply be quiet.

If you value your friend or your friendship, you can choose not to gossip. If you don't, it will eventually break up your friendship and you may lose that person as a part of your life forever. Also, have some tact in what you choose to address to your friends face. Your friend should feel that with you by their side, they are able to face the worst things in life; versus feeling that having you by their side will expose them to the worst experiences in life.

What if you are gossiping or being gossiped about?

There is a childhood game we played in kindergarten where the teacher would sit everyone around in a circle. She would whisper in the first child's ear a sentence like – *I like cherry pies from the corner store*. The child would then whisper in the next kid's ear what they heard, and the process repeated until the end. The very last student would verbally speak what they hear aloud for the entire class to hear, and oftentimes it was nothing similar to what was initially said. It usually ends up being something completely different like – *"I like grape eyes on a piano seat.*

Adults many times communicate and disseminate information incorrectly in the same way. In other words, if you are at the end of the rumor mill don't believe everything you hear. Carefully weigh and examine what others tell you and choose to communicate directly with your friend about it. Assumptions can fester and unnecessarily destroy any relationship if they are not discussed openly and honestly.

Choose friends who you, and everyone else they interact with, can trust. How they treat others is an indication of how they will likely at some point treat you. Remember that your tongue can be a sharp blade that can cut and destroy your relationships.

When you feel angry, irritated, frustrated, discontented, or impatient concerning your own life, choose to focus on *what you can do* with what you currently have to take positive action toward a goal in your life. It will cut down on the insecurity and stress you feel that causes you to gossip about others. It will also eliminate the time and energy you have to speak negatively of others.

Don't wound or harm your friends because of what is going on in your own life. Always watch what you say and think before you speak. Be cognizant of the impact your words have on the people around you. Figure out the words you can say to be a healing, uniting force in the lives of your friends and loved ones.

Make sure the words you speak and course of action you take are wise and that you would not be ashamed for anyone in your life to know about them. In doing so you can empower yourself to build a better life and take away the power of others who choose to waste their time gossiping about or around you.

Live that you wouldn't be ashamed to sell the family parrot to the town gossip.
~Will Rogers

Gossip is one of the horrible aspects of life and human interaction, that is not likely to completely go away or disappear anytime soon. There will always be someone who is wasting their time, and discontent or bitter because they are not accomplishing their own goals or living their dreams.

You can make your relationships and the world a better place simply by keeping your opinion about other people and their lives to yourself and choosing to not spread, engage in or listen to gossip. When you feel yourself absorbed in the gossiping words of someone else, or hear yourself repeating gossip to someone else, stop it. Walk away or hang up the phone and go work on a life goal. Figure out what enormous, amazing, outstanding impact you can make on the world around you.

Choosing not to gossip brings about peace in your

life. You will have much less drama by not engaging in this behavior than you will if you choose to participate. Being silent instead will pave the way for you to use your time more wisely and experience much more joy and peace throughout your life journey. Life can be difficult enough without you adding to someone else's stress levels or your own by spending your time gossiping.

Self reflective questions:
- Who, if anyone, have you recently gossiped about? If so, why did you do it?
- What are you hurting about?
- What in your own life are you lacking or fearing that caused you to pick that topic or person to talk about?
- How could you have made better use of your time?
- What cause or purpose is important to you?
- What are your goals and dreams?
- What are you doing to work toward them?

Commandment IX
Thou shalt listen

Commandment IX - Thou shalt listen

The most called-upon prerequisite of a friend is an accessible ear.
~Maya Angelou

Learning to listen to others is an important skill worth cultivating if you desire to have strong, lasting relationships. The Greek philosopher Epictetus stated, *"God gave man two ears but only one mouth that he might hear twice as much as he speaks."* Possessing great communication skills has much more to do with the ability to listen than it does with the ability to speak.

The ability to listen to one another helps to establish a strong foundation for your friendship to be built upon. Choosing to listen will help you gain a greater understanding about the life experience of your friend, what they have been through, and how they feel, thus improving and strengthening your bond.

Active listening is one way to enhance each of your friendships. It requires you to be conscious, deliberate and intentional. It calls for you to be attentive, observant and courteous in order to hear what those who are speaking are expressing to you. To be a good listener, you have to pay attention to someone outside of yourself, your own thoughts and the next words you are going to say.

People know if you have been listening and actually heard what they have said. They can hear whether or not your response was pre-formatted regardless of what came out of their mouth next. There is a discernible difference between someone who gives an orchestrated response versus one that genuinely takes heed to what they have heard.

It does not feel good when you know someone is not

listening to you. Through their actions they demonstrate that they believe their life, thoughts, words, opinions, and feelings are more important than yours. Therefore, do all you can to consciously improve your listening skills and give focused attention to the words of your friends during your conversations. Not doing so may eventually cause you to hear less and less from your friends as they progress into relationships where they are heard.

Silence…

There is a proverbial phrase that speech is silver, silence is golden. There is great wisdom that resides in silence. It allows you to be observant and grants you the ability to carefully assess a situation. Henri Nouwen stated, "The friend who can be silent with us in a moment of despair or confusion, who can stay with us in an hour of grief and bereavement, who can tolerate not knowing... not healing, not curing... that is a friend who cares."

Chances are when your friends call you regarding a situation they are dealing with; a silent mouth and *listening* ear may be what they need the most. Many times this silence will allow them to sort out their issues and find their own solution to the problem. Even if they need your help in finding a solution, sometimes a moment of silence is the wisest way to allow the answer to come.

Listen with an open heart and mind without jumping to conclusions or finishing someone's thought. Wisdom is best shared in a loving, calm, caring, kind, patient manner. Allow someone to express their feelings and when the time comes they can glean wisdom from the life experiences and opinions you choose to share. Wait until they ask for your input, and then interject to provide them with any wisdom, knowledge, intelligence, and life experiences you possess to help them.

*True friendship comes when silence between two
people is comfortable.
~Dave Tyson Gentry*

You know you've found a true friend when you can be silent when you're together and neither of you are agonizingly uncomfortable. You can have a moment of silence on the phone with them and it is not painful, and you are not scrambling for the next words to say to fill the void. This nonverbal bond allows you to communicate during situations without saying a word and know what one another are thinking.

Silence can be a beautiful thing for many reasons. It allows you to not only be a better listener, but is also an indicator of the strength of your friendship or relationship with that person. When you two can be quiet with or around one another and still enjoy one another's company, you know you've got something special. Hold onto, treat well, and treasure the friend you have found in them.

Benefits of listening...

Listening is a vital skill in beginning, maintaining, healing, and strengthening relationships. It is also a protective barrier within relationships because it is one of the few ways you can truly be informed of and discern who a person is. By simply closing your mouth and opening your ears you will be able to see the motives of others, and what they are thinking, feeling, or planning. Thus listening is a vital habit to develop.

Truly hearing the words and observing the actions of others helps you to see what lies ahead for you in the relationship. People will tell you exactly who they are, what they want, and what their true intentions are if you will just be quiet, patient and listen. Listening helps you to become a better friend, and also protect your own life, health, emotions and spirit.

Listening not only helps you strengthen the relationships you already have, but it also helps you start new ones. Most people absolutely love for someone to take interest in their life, thoughts, opinions, and feelings. Therefore, take a few moments each day to engage others in conversation. Let them speak and respond to the questions you ask, and then simply listen. It makes people feel good for someone to care and ask about what they have to say, even if it is coming from a stranger.

When you meet new people, simply ask something about their life, something positive you notice about them, their occupation or even how their day is going. Then listen to their response. Most people will go on talking beyond answering your specific question because it is challenging these days to find a plethora of individuals who truly care what is happening in your life.

If they ask you questions in return, then great. If not, just give them a chance to get a little bit of positive attention or maybe even exhortation from you for the day. They will remember you for it. If you recall and let them know you remembered the details of the conversation the next time you run into one another, you may be on the verge of establishing a new friendship. By constantly stepping outside of yourself and being concerned about others, you will be able to build friendships and relationships throughout your life.

Just to clarify, this is not to say you have to or should badger people with questions. Simply show an interest in their life by taking the time to get to know them. You don't have to ask everything about them within 30 seconds of meeting them. Ask something simple, let them respond, and listen!

Mannerisms…

Most times, your mannerisms speak louder than your words. Therefore, you should begin to pay great attention to what your faces and body language are saying to your friends as you are listening. Establish eye contact as they speak to you to convey you are interested in what they are saying. Don't interrupt while they talk. Avoid fidgeting and looking around the room at anyone and everything else or worse, having your eyes glued to your phone or other devices.

Also, take time to notice their facial expressions, mannerisms, vocal tone and body language as they speak. You can better discern what your friend is feeling and what they may need from you when you do. As your friend speaks, plan to pause and let silence set in for a second before you speak to ensure that you have heard what they have said.

Instead of responding with your opinion all the time, consider responding with intelligent, kind-hearted, well-meaning questions. Repeat back to them what they have said to let them know you were listening. Step outside of yourself, consider what they want, think and feel. Ask yourself *why* they may want, think or feel that way. As you exercise great listening skills, your friend will be able to release what's been happening with them and likely come to a conclusion concerning what they should do about it on their own.

When your friend is really going through something in life, simply be available as a shoulder to lean on and a listening ear. Be their support structure. Becoming a great listener will help you begin to build new friendships and significantly improve the ones you already have. Your loving or kind presence and moments of silence are many times the greatest gifts you can give to someone. Choose today to silence your tongue, open your ears and display to your friends the genuine care, powerful love, and deep compassion that lies within you. As a result, your friendships will flourish in ways you never imagined.

Silences make the real conversations between friends. Not the saying but the never needing to say is what counts.
~Margaret Lee Runbeck

Question:
- How often do you stop talking to listen to others around you?
- Who in your life can you have comfortable moments of silence with?
- Who in your life do you need to pause and listen to?
- What can you do to improve your listening skills (and body mannerisms while listening) to enhance your relationships?

Commandment X
Thou shalt forgive and apologize

Commandment X - Thou shalt forgive and apologize

You can always tell a real friend: when you've made a fool of yourself he doesn't feel you've done a permanent job.
~Laurence J. Peter

When someone does something harmful to your mind, body or spirit, forgiving them can be a difficult task. Oftentimes, forgiveness is one of the most challenging things to learn and master in life. Responding to hate, inconsiderateness, or maliciousness with kindness and love requires great spiritual maturity and emotional strength.

Why forgive?

Forgiving is a difficult task for many people. It is easy to simply tell someone to forgive, but most situations that warrant forgiveness bring about apprehension. However, it is beneficial to get beyond these reservations as it can allow healing to occur. In many instances, the love and wisdom you exercise in forgiving someone who harmed you can help them grow emotionally and spiritually as well. It enables you to hold onto your power and reestablishes a sense of peace and joy within your own heart. Further, forgiving others keeps you from harboring hateful feelings. When you fail to forgive, resentment usually builds within you until you inflict more harm to yourself than the person who initially harmed or offended you.

Resentment is like drinking poison and waiting for it to kill your enemy.
~Nelson Mandela.

THE 10 COMMANDMENTS OF FRIENDSHIP

To build, develop, and maintain friendships, the act of forgiveness is something you must learn. Your friends are not going to be perfect or do everything you would like them to do all the time; and most likely they feel the same regarding you. The truth is we are all human and make mistakes. Throughout your friendship there will be words said or actions taken, knowingly or unknowingly, that will hurt others. Thus learning how to forgive is paramount to sustaining relationships.

When you choose not to forgive, you allow the issue to fester within you and remain miserable while everyone else around you, including the person who hurt you, moves on with their lives. Try not to put your life on hold because someone did something foolish, inconsiderate, or hurtful to you.

Forgiveness unties, releases, and frees you. If you have been hurt or offended, acknowledge what has occurred, forgive what others have done to you, and move on to experience a successful, joy-filled life. By choosing to be positive and selecting the high road, you pave the way for positive relationships in the future.

The possibility of positive experiences and people entering your life is much more likely when you let go and release these negative thoughts, language, and energy. Choosing not to forgive builds up negative feelings of resentment that will block and hinder blessings. In turn, this prevents great relationships you may not even know you are missing out on.

To forgive is to set a prisoner free and discover that the prisoner was you.
~Lewis B. Smedes

Salvaging friendships…

When a friend has a grudge against you, go to your friend and make things right. True friendships are worth salvaging. You will have more peace making amends than harboring resentment and strife within your heart. When you know in your heart that you have done all the good you can to fix, salvage, or repair a relationship it is easier to move forward with your life no matter what the outcome may be.

To be good friends, you must learn to be considerate of one another. Choose to be understanding and spend your time cultivating a life full of positive experiences and fond memories. In doing so you create a common purpose to reunite your friendship during challenging times. When one of you has unintentionally inflicted harm on another, it will be much easier to mend the relationship and reunite if you have positive experiences and memories to draw and rebuild from.

It is easier to forgive an enemy than to forgive a friend.
~William Blake

Most people expect horrible, hateful behavior from their enemies. Conversely, they expect their friends to love them, care about them and conduct themselves accordingly. When you hurt your friend, it feels like a debilitating punch to their abdomen. It is more challenging to cope with a friend backstabbing you than to deal with negative, self-serving behavior from one thousand enemies.

If a friend hurts you, be honest and tell them, then work it out. It's not impossible for you to reconnect with a true friend. If you did something to damage the relationship, figure out exactly what it is, apologize, and do what you can to fix it. If they refuse to hear you, see if you can interject a mediator who can help bridge that communication gap. At least give it an attempt.

If you have exhausted all resources and they still refuse to listen to you after you sincerely apologize, then proceed forward with your life with no further animosity or regrets. Your positive actions and lessons you've learned from previous mistakes will open the door for other people to enter and bless your life.

Your willingness to apologize may soften the heart of your friend and you may be able to reconnect and rebuild at a later date when they are ready, willing, and able to trust you again. Don't give up on the friendship altogether. Simply sow positive words and actions toward others until what you sow returns to you in the form of beautiful, strong, lasting friendships.

Ending relationships…

Relationships come to an end for many reasons. Sometimes miscommunication can be the culprit in damaging relationships. Words can be easily misinterpreted, even if it was not the intention of the other person. In contrast there are other situations where this is not the case, and what you saw and heard should be taken for face value.

Faced with this predicament, it is okay to end a friendship or relationship that is abusive, negative or toxic. You do not have to try to hold onto what is clearly harmful, not working, or simply bad for your life. When it is necessary for you to exit a friendship for the sake of salvaging your sanity, emotional, physical or spiritual well-being, try your best to end it on a positive note. The manner in which your relationships end, will determine your ability to move into healthy, positive, strong relationships in your future. Make sure that if or when you need to walk away, that you can do so without regrets.

The offended…

If you are the one who has been offended, take a moment to really assess if the offense is really worth ending the relationship. Maybe even give it a day or two and see if you still feel the same tomorrow. Try not to be the type of person who gets offended easily and takes everything personal. Life is short and spending your days being offended can definitely be a waste of your time.

When someone hurts you, take a moment to assess the situation. Talk to them and see if you even have a valid reason for being offended. Many times you will see the underlying reasoning and intentions behind what is upsetting you was not the intent of the person you were offended by. Ask them what their intentions were.

Learn to trust your friend's heart. If they are a good friend, and you have a long history together their heart is likely in the right place. There may be something going on in their life that is difficult and challenging for them that has absolutely nothing to do with you. If your relationship is valuable, you will learn to forgive. Sometimes being a good friend means letting some minor offenses go for the best interest of everyone involved.

You also need to learn how to set healthy boundaries and standards for yourself. If negative harmful behavior toward you becomes a pattern, then it may be time to reassess the friendship and draw new boundary lines. These safeguards prevent others from abusing your mind, body, spirit or emotional state. Sometimes love means walking away until a person gets their conduct and life together. It doesn't mean you don't love and care for your friend. It means you love them enough to inform them that their behavior is not okay, and that you love yourself enough to protect your life, health, and emotional state.

Ask yourself the best way to handle the issue or problem with your friend. Don't wallow in a negative situation and allow hurt feelings and disagreements to fester. Life is too short to be petty or too afraid to address valid concerns. Be an adult and confront the situation, talk through it, forgive each other then move on. Making enemies requires too much energy. Enter each situation determined to forgive and let it go. Going forward, agree to make wiser choices for your future, your own sanity, your peace, and restoration of your joy.

Forgiving an offense can definitely make your relationship stronger and allow you to develop a deeper bond moving forward, as it is a true demonstration of love and kindness. Don't take small things too seriously and choose your battles wisely. Friends are able to love one another through and in spite of imperfections.

However, true friends will not knowingly, continually hurt one another either. Always remember that forgiving someone and repeatedly giving them access to continue to do it over and over again are two separate things. Discern what is actually happening and decide where your relationship stands.

How to ask for and accept forgiveness…

If you have done something to destroy a friendship that you would like to see restored, reach out and apologize in person, by phone, e-mail or letter. Let the person know you are sorry for whatever it is that you have done. Ask how they are doing now. If they respond, listen. Most likely they will communicate their needs.

You can restore a relationship with a long-lost friend, but it may take time for healing and forgiveness to occur. Don't expect people to just get over everything you have done. They can forgive, but it may take a little bit of time to rebuild the trust that once existed. If you are the one who has violated their trust, then you need to allow them whatever amount of time they need to determine when that trust has been restored. You will allow them whatever amount of space or time they need if you want the relationship to be repaired.

Simply let them know you apologize and are there for them if they ever need you or desire to have you as a part of their life. Check up on them every now and then (if they are accepting of your presence in their life). Don't try to force your way back into anyone's life or you will fail miserably. Be a friend, give them space, and they may become your friend once again in the future.

If not, it is okay. Once again, allow the situation to be a learning lesson as you move forward with your life and develop new friendships. You will have at least exited on a more positive note as opposed to their last memory of you being a harmful act.

Ten steps to deal with a friend who has hurt you…

1. *Address the issue -* Let them know exactly what they have done to hurt you and how you feel about it. Your friend cannot read your mind about what you want, need or are offended about. Don't lie, cover up, or hide how you feel. Never say it's okay or alright if it is not.
2. *Make it private* - Discuss the matter in private between you and whoever hurt or offended you. Don't ever do it publicly or in front of a group of people as it will only add fuel to the fire that already exists.

The 10 Commandments Of Friendship

3. ***Listen*** – Momentarily place your feelings aside, and listen to your friend's explanation of what they did and why they did it. It is possible that you may have misunderstood their intent. Hear them out and then figure out if you still feel offended.
4. ***Consider your imperfections*** - Understand that you are not perfect either. Remember how you felt when you did something to hurt someone else and wanted their forgiveness. Or think about how you would feel if you were the one who committed the offense and were sorry for it.
5. ***Reminisce*** - Remember the good times that you and your friend had together in the past and what you appreciated about them being in your life.
6. ***Consider your health*** - Forgive your friend for the sake of your own health and future. Don't harbor negative feelings in your mind, body, and spirit. Forgive, grant pardon, cease to blame or feel resentment against them, and be merciful for your own well-being.
7. ***Set boundaries*** – Establish clear boundaries and inform your friend of how you want to proceed forward with your life and the relationship.
8. ***No drama*** – Forgive, let it go, and move on. The choice to forgive is always totally up to you. After you forgive, don't keep revisiting the event or your feelings once it has been discussed and you verbally expressed that you forgave them. Rehashing hurtful situations from the past can be harmful to you as well as the person that harmed you.
9. ***Forgive anyway*** - If your friend never expresses remorse or apologizes for what you feel they have

done to hurt you, forgive them anyway. Forgiveness is not just for them, it is for you as well. Try to remember that people who hurt other people are usually in great pain and turmoil themselves.
10. ***Move on*** - Don't revisit the past and keep retelling the story. Let it go, let it go, let it go. You can learn the lesson and then move forward with your life. There are too many goals and dreams you can still accomplish and too much exists ahead of you to waste time on the past.

One who looks for a friend without faults will have none.
~Hasidic Saying

Steps to repairing a relationship with a friend you hurt…

- ***Listen*** - Listen to your friend's thoughts and feelings about what you have done that hurt them. Then think through why you did what you did and what caused you to do it. Be honest with yourself so you can heal whatever is going on within you, in order to not make the same mistake going forward into the future.
- ***Apologize*** - Apologize to your friend for what you have done, but say what you mean. If you are not sorry, don't apologize. However if your action hurt your friend, you may want to reevaluate why you are not remorseful. No one can force you to examine yourself and your life but it is wise to do so. If you are sincerely sorry for what you've done, demonstrate the sincerity of your

apology to your friend through your future actions. Don't apologize and then set them up to be hurt again when you never planned on changing, growing, or improving your behavior. Give them an opportunity to move on with their life verses being hurt again.
- ***Explain why*** - If you truly are sorry for the offense, explain to your friend why you did what you did, what you were wrong about, and what you are willing to change proceeding forward.
- ***Be accountable*** - Take responsibility for what you did or for your part in whatever happened.
- ***Show gratitude*** - Express your appreciation for your friend's forgiveness, willingness to listen, and presence in your life.
- ***Give space*** - Give your friend time, space, and an opportunity to heal, forgive, and trust you again. Be patient. You are the one who offended or hurt your friend. You don't get to make demands about when or how they forgive you.
- ***Change*** - Follow through on actually being a better person and friend moving forward. Don't go back to the same behavior that hurt them as you two proceed forward with your friendship.

Wishing to be friends is quick work, but friendship is a slow ripening fruit.
~Aristotle

Life can be a challenging voyage. True friends are

rare and worth keeping along your way. When you have true friends by your side, it makes life seem much less difficult to bear. Life passes by quickly, therefore there is no time to waste in mishandling your friendships and relationships. Don't complicate things unnecessarily. Decide what you want, fix and repair what you can, and move forward with positive intentions for healthy relationships in your future.

Keep life as simple as you can and try not to take too many things to heart. Forgive what hurts your heart and figure out what you can learn from it. There is a silver lining in every situation. Even in bad situations, we can grow and it can lead to a better future.

Keep your focus on the big picture and sum total of your life instead of one hurtful moment or day. Develop and maintain strong, deep friendships versus superficial associations as they are a huge part of what makes life worth living. Repair and nurture the precious relationships and rare friendships you have been given. Appreciate, value, love and care for the friends you have been blessed with thus far, as well as those you will meet in the future.

Hold a true friend with both your hands.
~Nigerian Proverb

Questions:
- Who has hurt, harmed, or offended you emotionally, physically, or spiritually?
- Who do you need to forgive?
- Who have you hurt, harmed or offended?
- Who do you need to apologize to? What do you need to apologize for?

The 10 Commandments Of Friendship

- How can you most sincerely express your regret and remorse for what you have done?
- What is the most loving way you can handle each of your friendships?
- Who do you need or desire to reconnect with?
- What is necessary to restore your relationship today?

Always Remember:

To a friend's house, the road is never long.
~Danish Proverb

A real friend is one who walks in when the rest of the world walks out.
~Walter Winchell

There is nothing on this earth more to be prized than true friendship.
~Thomas Aquinas

10 Commandments of Friendship
Conclusion

CONCLUSION

Some people never get to experience the many blessings that come along with a true, strong, lasting friendship. Possibly because they don't understand the purpose of friendships, or how to manage them properly. Friends can make your life journey a more rewarding one, however you must first learn how to interact within them before you can reap the rewards. If you have read this far in this book, you are now equipped to build new friendships, better manage the ones you already have, and repair the ones that may be damaged.

When you adhere to the principles within the *Ten Commandments of Friendship*, people in your life will have a higher regard and respect for you. You will be honored by those who love and care about you, and possibly those on your job and in your community for how you carry yourself. People will notice a change in you. When you speak, people will desire to listen and respect what you have to say. They will know and trust that the words that you speak are out of love and be more likely to listen because they trust you. Your good, kind, loving, giving reputation will precede you and provide you with favor with others in your life.

By applying these simple relationship principles to your daily life, you will be recognized and celebrated for helping others in need and being fair to everyone you come in contact with. Your care for others around you will cause you to champion their cause, problem or plight. These characteristics are what make people want to be in your presence.

In other words, there are a lot of benefits to being a good friend. Learning how to manage and maintain friendships will bring about peace which will deeply enrich your life on the earth. To have this experience, do all you can to fix, repair, heal, and rebuild whatever friendships and relationships exist in your life. If you and your friends are both striving to be great friends and to fulfill the great plans and purposes of your lives, this should not be difficult. Delight in the presence of your friends and sow positive words and actions into your friendships. After all, they are one of the greatest blessings that you can experience in life. Treasure, nurture and value them!

ABOUT THE AUTHORS

Jerome and Marla McCarthy have been long-time friends and partners in life, marriage, parenting, and business. They have authored several books and resources such as *Marriage as Advertised*, *Enhancing Your Journey*, *Rose from the Basement*, and *Create the Life You Want Now*. Together they have co-authored titles such as *The 10 Commandments of Friendship* and *The 30 Day Intimacy Challenge for Married Couples.* As the founders of The Real Life Series Publishing Company LLC., they strive to provide reading and multimedia material to encourage and bless the lives of others.

When not spending time with his family, Jerome mentors young men and volunteers as a youth football and basketball coach. Under his coaching and tutelage, many young people have developed a new found love of sports, as well as increased levels of confidence and personal responsibility. Marla is a life and relationship coach, certified personal trainer, weight loss specialist, and youth sport fitness coordinator. She has a passion for helping others break what appear to be limiting factors off their lives to develop a life of total health, love, peace, joy and personal empowerment.

Jerome and Marla currently reside in the Dallas-Fort Worth, TX area with their six sons and one daughter.

ALSO AVAILABLE FROM THE REAL LIFE SERIES PUBLISHING CO.

Marriage As Advertised
by Jerome J. McCarthy
Fiction/Novel
ISBN-13: 978-0-9800083-9-5

**Enhancing Your Journey:
Quarterly Prayer Journal**
by Marla A. McCarthy
Non-Fiction/Self-Help
ISBN-13: 978-0-9800083-5-7

Rose From The Basement
by Jerome J. McCarthy
Fiction/Novel
ISBN-13: 978-0-9800083-4-0

**Create The Life You Want Now:
Quarterly Goal Journal**
by Marla A. McCarthy
Non-Fiction/Self-Help
ISBN-13: 978-0-9800083-3-3

The 30 Day Intimacy Challenge for Married Couples
by Jerome J. McCarthy, Marla A. McCarthy
Non-Fiction/Self-Help
ISBN-13: 978-0-9800083-7-1

Loving Me:
A Guide to Renewing Your Mind, Body and Spirit
by Marla A. McCarthy
Non-Fiction/Self-Help
ISBN-13: 978-0-9800083-0-2

R.O.S.E.
Raising Our Standards and Expectations:
Transforming Your Ability To Handle Relationships
by Marla A. McCarthy
Non-Fiction/Self-Help
ISBN-13: 978-0-9800083-8-8

Inquires should be addressed to:
The Real Life Series Publishing Co., LLC
PO BOX 1563, Keller, TX 76244-1896

www.TheRealLifeSeries.com
info@thereallifeseries.com

www.ingramcontent.com/pod-product-compliance
Lightning Source LLC
Chambersburg PA
CBHW051437290426
44109CB00016B/1594